ADHD Women & Relationships

Empower Your Growth, Master
Relationships, Nurture Emotional Bonds
and Executive Functioning Skills as a
Women Thriving With ADHD

Ivy Castillo

Thank You!

As a token of our appreciation, scan the QR code below to download the Laugh-a-licious Workbook Companion—your fun partner in self-discovery and growth!

We hope this workbook brings you joy! If you have any questions or want to stay updated, feel free to reach out at hello@ivycastillo.com

We'd Love Your Feedback! Your thoughts help us and guide others to valuable insights.

Thank you for being part of our community!

Table of Contents

Introduction

The rain fell relentlessly outside, drumming against the windowpane as if in perfect sync with the chaos inside my mind. It was one of those evenings when my ADHD seemed to have a spotlight, magnifying every distraction, and scattering my thoughts in all directions.

I sat across from my partner, trying desperately to focus on our conversation. Amidst the symphony of rain and bustling café noises, my mind was a whirlwind, snatching thoughts like butterflies and releasing them before I could make sense of them. My partner's face blurred at times, lost in the fog of my mental restlessness.

As I watched them recount stories from their day, I marveled at how effortlessly they seemed to navigate the social dance of conversation. Meanwhile, my attention darted between the music playing softly in the background, the vibrant colors on the walls, and the waitstaff hastening around, each carrying a tray of steaming cups. It felt as if I were in a labyrinth of sensory overload, unable to find the way out.

Without realizing it, I found my gaze fixated on a group of friends huddled together nearby, laughter echoing through the air. I suddenly felt an overwhelming guilt as I realized my attention had wandered. The smile on my partner's face faded, replaced by a flicker of concern.

"I'm so sorry," I stammered, desperately trying to grasp onto the swiftly escaping conversation. "It's just... my mind... it's like a runaway train sometimes."

A soft, understanding smile graced my partner's lips as they reached out to hold my hand. Their voice, full of compassion, broke through the noise. "I know, love. Your beautiful mind dances to its own rhythm, and I'm here to dance with you."

In that moment, I knew that true connection wasn't about finding the perfect listener or mastering the art of focus. It was about finding someone who embraced the intricacies of my ADHD and loved me not despite them but because of them. It was about finding patience, empathy, and understanding in a world that often seemed to demand conformity. In that embrace of understanding, I witnessed a glimpse of what true connection could be. It was a moment of acceptance where my partner recognized that my ADHD was not a flaw or a hindrance but a unique aspect of who I am. And with their unwavering support, I began to realize that true compatibility and fulfillment in relationships extend far beyond what society deems "normal" or "ideal."

This book, "ADHD Women and Relationships," is like that understanding partner. It is here to hold your hand through the twists and turns of navigating love, intimacy, and companionship as an ADHD woman. This isn't a guidebook that attempts to mold you into someone you're not, but rather a safe space that celebrates the strengths and quirks that make you beautifully and authentically yourself.

Within these pages, you'll find stories, insights, and practical strategies that honor the intricacies of ADHD and explore the complexities that arise in relationships. We'll delve into the unique challenges we face as ADHD women and explore how we can build and maintain fulfilling connections with our partners, family, friends, and even within ourselves.

Just as my partner's understanding allowed me to feel seen and supported, this book is here to offer that same understanding and encouragement. It recognizes the daily battles we fight within our own minds—the whirlwind of racing thoughts, the struggle to stay present, and the overwhelming emotions that can sometimes overwhelm us. But it also acknowledges the tremendous strengths and gifts that often accompany our ADHD, such as creativity, intuition, and a vibrant zest for life. Through real-life experiences and expert advice, we'll explore effective communication strategies, emotional regulation techniques, and ways to navigate common challenges like forgetfulness, impulsivity, and time management issues. We'll dig deeper into how ADHD can affect our self-esteem, intimacy, and the dynamics of our relationships. And most importantly, we'll discover ways to foster understanding, empathy, and growth both within ourselves and in our relationships.

As my partner reminded me that our dance together was not meant to follow a set rhythm, this book emphasizes the importance of embracing our own unique dance in relationships. It encourages us to communicate our needs and challenges openly while also learning to understand and appreciate the needs and perspectives of our loved ones. This is a book that reminds us that love is not about fitting into molds or ticking off boxes but rather about finding someone who celebrates our differences and dances beside us, even when the steps seem uncertain.

As we embark on this journey together, I invite you to let go of society's expectations and embrace the beauty of your own neurodivergent self. Let's celebrate our remarkable strengths and navigate the challenges that come with ADHD. Let's explore the intricate tapestry of relationships and find the connections that bring us joy, contentment, and fulfillment.

Within these pages, we'll learn to rewrite the narrative, transforming the struggles of ADHD into stepping stones towards deeper intimacy, stronger connections, and a love that lights up our lives.

Chapter 1:

Understanding ADHD in Women

Meet Sarah, a successful professional in her 30s. On the surface, she exudes confidence and competence, effortlessly managing her responsibilities. However, beneath her composed exterior lies a constant struggle—a battle against the invisible forces of ADHD that have shaped her life. Despite her achievements, Sarah often finds herself grappling with missed deadlines, forgotten appointments, and a nagging feeling of being overwhelmed. Her journey is a testament to the hidden complexities of ADHD in women.

For years, Sarah struggled to understand why she felt different from her peers. She noticed that she had trouble staying focused, frequently losing track of time, and getting easily distracted. While her colleagues seemed to effortlessly juggle multiple tasks, Sarah found herself overwhelmed by even the simplest of to-do lists. It wasn't until she stumbled upon an article about ADHD in women that she began to connect the dots.

Sarah discovered that ADHD in women often presents itself differently than in men. Rather than the stereotypical image of hyperactive boys, women with ADHD often exhibit more internalized symptoms. They may struggle with organization, time management, and maintaining attention, leading to a constant sense of chaos and frustration.

As Sarah delved deeper into her research, she realized that the unique challenges faced by women with ADHD often go unnoticed or misattributed. Many women, like Sarah, have spent years feeling misunderstood and dismissed, their struggles brushed off as mere forgetfulness or lack of discipline. The invisible nature of ADHD in women can make it difficult for them to seek help or receive the support they need.

Sarah's story is just one example of the countless women who navigate the complexities of ADHD every day. In this chapter, we will explore the distinct experiences, challenges, and strengths of women with ADHD. By shedding light on this often-overlooked topic, we hope to gain a better understanding of ourselves and learn how to empower ourselves to embrace our unique neurodiversity and thrive in a world that often fails to recognize our struggles.

Symptoms and Characteristics of ADHD

When it comes to ADHD, it's like stepping into a vibrant and unpredictable world where the mind dances to its own rhythm. This condition manifests in a variety of ways, each with its own set of characteristics that make each person's experience unique. So, let's take a closer look at how ADHD shows up and the specific traits that define it, all while keeping a touch of humor and insight.

One of the hallmark features of ADHD is difficulty with attention and focus. It's like trying to catch a butterfly with a net made of spaghetti—the mind flits from one thought to another, making it challenging to stay on track. You might find yourself easily distracted by the smallest of things, like a passing bird or an interesting conversation in the next room. It's as if your attention has a mind of its own, wandering off on its own adventures.

Another characteristic of ADHD is impulsivity, the tendency to act on impulse without thinking through the consequences. It's like having an enthusiastic puppy inside your brain, always ready to pounce on the next exciting idea or opportunity. You might find yourself blurting out thoughts without filtering them, making decisions on a whim, or engaging in risky behaviors without fully considering the potential outcomes. It's a constant battle between the desire for instant gratification and the need for thoughtful reflection.

Hyperactivity is another aspect of ADHD that often comes to mind. It's like having an internal motor that's always revving, making it difficult to sit still or stay quiet. You might find yourself fidgeting, tapping your foot, or constantly shifting in your seat. It's as if your body has its own rhythm—a beat that needs to be expressed through movement. While hyperactivity is more commonly associated with ADHD in children, it can also persist into adulthood, albeit in a more subdued form.

But what about the specific characteristics of ADHD in women? Well, here's where things get interesting. Women with ADHD often experience their symptoms in a more internalized and less overt manner. Instead of the stereotypical image of the hyperactive boy, women may struggle with restlessness and a constant feeling of being overwhelmed. It's like having a whirlwind of thoughts and responsibilities swirling inside your mind, making it challenging to find a sense of calm.

Emotional dysregulation is another characteristic that sets women with ADHD apart. It's like riding an emotional rollercoaster, with highs and lows that can leave you feeling like you're on a wild ride. You might experience intense emotions that seem to come out of nowhere, like a sudden burst of tears or a surge of anger. It can be confusing and exhausting, both for yourself and those around you. But amidst the chaos, there's also a depth of feeling and empathy that can be a source of strength.

Women with ADHD confront distinct challenges in organization and time management. While men may exhibit outward disarray with cluttered desks and chaotic schedules, women often present a more polished facade. Beneath this exterior, however, lies an ongoing struggle to maintain control. Many women find themselves relying on intricate systems—like color-coded calendars and comprehensive to-do lists—to navigate daily tasks and keep the chaos at bay, much like conducting a symphony amidst constant disarray.

As we explore the specific characteristics of ADHD, it's important to remember that everyone's experience is different. ADHD is a complex and multifaceted condition that manifests uniquely in each individual. By understanding these characteristics, we can gain insight into our own strengths and challenges and find strategies to navigate the world with greater ease.

Okay, so while we've had a good laugh about the quirks and challenges of ADHD, it's important to recognize that this condition can manifest differently in men and women. Just like two sides of the same coin, ADHD presents its unique face to each gender, with its own set of characteristics and complexities. So, let's take a closer look at how ADHD dances to a different beat in the world of men and women.

In the realm of ADHD, men often take the spotlight with their more outwardly visible symptoms. They may exhibit hyperactivity, restlessness, and impulsivity that can make them the life of the party or the bane of their teachers' existence. Their energy seems boundless, like a firecracker that never fails to ignite. It's as if they have an internal motor that's always running at full speed.

But what about the ladies? Well, it turns out that women with ADHD often have a different story to tell. For them, ADHD often wears a cloak of invisibility, hiding beneath the surface and presenting itself in more subtle ways. Instead of bouncing off the walls, women may struggle with internal restlessness, feeling like they're constantly juggling a million thoughts and responsibilities in their minds. It's like having a mental circus, complete with tightrope walking and plate spinning, all while maintaining a graceful facade.

One of the key gender-specific symptoms that women with ADHD often face is the challenge of emotional regulation. It's like riding an emotional rollercoaster, with highs and lows that can leave you feeling exhausted and overwhelmed. You may find yourself crying at a heartwarming commercial one moment and then laughing uncontrollably at a silly joke the next. It's a whirlwind of emotions that can leave those around you scratching their heads in confusion.

In addition to emotional fluctuations, women with ADHD frequently face challenges in effectively managing their time. While they often appear organized on the surface, the reality can be much different. This dynamic highlights the significant pressure they feel to project an image of control, even when they are contending with persistent distractions. To cope, many turn to innovative strategies, utilizing tools like planners or apps to streamline their tasks. Through these tailored organizational approaches, they seek to cultivate a sense of order and balance in their lives, reflecting their resilience and adaptability in navigating the complexities of ADHD.

These gender-specific differences in ADHD symptoms highlight the importance of recognizing and understanding the unique challenges faced by women. By shedding light on these nuances, we can provide better support, guidance, and resources for women with ADHD. It's about embracing the diversity within the ADHD community and ensuring that everyone's voice is heard.

Dispelling the Myths and Misconceptions

I'm sure that you have heard a lot of things about you and your ADHD. Maybe you've been told that you're just scatterbrained or spacey, or that ADHD is something you should have outgrown by now. Well, it's time to set the record straight, don't you think? Let's unpack some of those myths and why they simply are not true.

Myth #1: *ADHD is only a problem for hyperactive kids.*

Contrary to popular belief, ADHD doesn't magically disappear when childhood ends. Many women continue to struggle with ADHD symptoms well into adulthood. It may manifest differently, though, often presenting as chronic forgetfulness, difficulty focusing, or chronic disorganization.

Myth #2: "ADHD is just an excuse for being lazy or scatterbrained."

Having ADHD is not synonymous with laziness or a lack of intelligence. In fact, people with ADHD often possess remarkable creativity and problem-solving skills. We may, however, struggle with executive functions such as planning, prioritizing, and organization. It's important to recognize that ADHD is a neurodevelopmental condition, not a character flaw.

Myth #3: "Women with ADHD can't be successful in their careers."

ADHD does not determine your potential for success. Numerous accomplished women in various fields thrive with ADHD. Many have developed coping mechanisms, found the right treatment plan, and harnessed the strengths that come with their condition. ADHD can even provide a unique perspective and drive for women pursuing their passions.

Myth #4: "Only children can have ADHD."

ADHD affects individuals of all ages, including women. While it is true that symptoms often emerge during childhood, it is equally possible for adults to receive an ADHD diagnosis. For some women, their symptoms may go undetected until later in life, when they face new challenges or heightened expectations.

Myth #5: "Women with ADHD are ditzy and forgetful."

Forgetfulness is not exclusive to women with ADHD, although they might struggle more with it. Distraction and difficulty maintaining focus can contribute to occasional forgetfulness. It's important to remember that forgetfulness is a symptom of the condition, not an inherent quality of the person.

Myth #6: "ADHD is caused by bad parenting or a lack of discipline."

ADHD is a neurological condition with genetic and environmental factors at play. It's not a result of poor parenting or a lack of discipline. Although structure and support are crucial for managing symptoms, external factors are not the cause of ADHD.

Myth #7: "ADHD medication turns you into a completely different person."

ADHD medication can be a valuable tool for managing symptoms, but it doesn't fundamentally change who you are as a person. Its purpose is to enhance focus and attention, allowing you to better navigate the aspects of your daily lives. Medication should always be prescribed and monitored by a medical professional to ensure the right dosage and approach for your unique case.

Impact of ADHD on Relationships: With Our Partners

Sarah's partner, John, feels frustrated and misunderstood when she forgets important dates or struggles with impulsivity. It's not uncommon for Sarah to unintentionally double-book plans or impulsively make decisions without considering the consequences. This often leads to tension and strain in their relationship, as John interprets these behaviors as a lack of care or thoughtfulness.

For instance, on their anniversary, Sarah forgot to make reservations at their favorite restaurant, leaving John disappointed and hurt. He wondered why she couldn't remember such an important date and asked if she truly valued their relationship. Similarly, Sarah's impulsive spending habits cause financial stress, as she often makes impromptu purchases without considering their budget or long-term goals. This leaves John feeling anxious and worried about their financial stability.

The truth, as it stands, is that these challenges in their relationship are not a reflection of Sarah's lack of love or commitment. Instead, they are manifestations of the impact that ADHD can have on her daily life. Sarah's forgetfulness and impulsivity are not intentional but rather symptoms of her ADHD. Understanding this can help John approach these situations with empathy and support rather than frustration and blame.

Here's the thing: Living with ADHD can present unique challenges in our romantic relationships that often leave both partners feeling vulnerable and misunderstood. The symptoms of ADHD, such as forgetfulness, impulsivity, and difficulty with time management, can create friction and strain in the connection between partners.

Forgetfulness, which is a common symptom of ADHD, can lead to missing important dates or commitments, leaving our partners feeling neglected or unimportant. It's not that we don't care about these occasions; our minds can simply become overwhelmed with the constant flow of thoughts and distractions. Our partners may interpret this forgetfulness as a lack of love or commitment, leading to feelings of frustration and hurt.

Impulsivity, another characteristic of ADHD, can also impact our romantic relationships. We may make impulsive decisions without fully considering the consequences, which can catch our partners off guard. This can lead to misunderstandings and disagreements, as our partners may question our judgment or commitment to the relationship. It's important for both partners to recognize that impulsivity is not a deliberate act of disregard but rather a manifestation of the challenges we face due to ADHD.

Additionally, the difficulties with time management that often accompany ADHD can strain our romantic relationships. We may struggle to balance responsibilities and maintain a sense of stability. Our partners may feel burdened by the additional responsibilities they have to take on due to our challenges with organization and planning. This imbalance can create resentment and frustration, eroding the foundation of trust and support in the relationship. We may also find it challenging to regulate our emotions, leading to heightened reactions or difficulty expressing ourselves calmly. This can make it difficult for our partners to understand or respond to our emotional fluctuations, leading to further strain in the relationship.

Impact of ADHD on Relationships

With Our Family

Sarah's family is gathered around the dinner table, ready to enjoy a delicious homemade meal. As they eagerly anticipate the first bite, Sarah suddenly realizes that she forgot a crucial ingredient for the recipe. With a sheepish grin, she exclaims, "Oops! Looks like we're having spaghetti without the sauce tonight!"

Her family bursts into laughter, accustomed to these unexpected twists that ADHD often brings to their lives. Her forgetfulness has become a running joke in the family, with each mishap turning into a memorable story to share during gatherings.

However, beneath the laughter lies a deeper impact on their family relationships. Sarah's ADHD-related challenges with organization and time management can create moments of frustration and stress. Her forgetfulness extends beyond missing ingredients for meals; it also means misplaced car keys, forgotten permission slips, and last-minute scrambles to find misplaced items.

These situations can lead to moments of tension and exasperation, as family members may struggle to understand why Sarah can't seem to keep track of things. Siblings may feel annoyed by the extra responsibilities they have to take on or the delays caused by Sarah's forgetfulness.

Yet, amidst the challenges, Sarah's family has learned to embrace the quirks that come with ADHD. They recognize that her forgetfulness is not a deliberate act but a manifestation of her unique brain wiring. They have developed strategies to support her, such as creating visual reminders, setting up designated spaces for important items, and practicing patience when things go awry.

In fact, Sarah's ADHD has also brought unexpected moments of joy and creativity to their family dynamic. Her hyperfocus, a common trait in individuals with ADHD, often leads to bursts of enthusiasm and passion for various hobbies or projects. Whether it's diving into a new artistic endeavor or exploring a fascinating topic, Sarah's family witnesses her infectious excitement and admires her ability to find joy in the smallest of things.

Through humor, understanding, and a willingness to adapt, her family has built a resilient bond that transcends the challenges of ADHD. They have learned to appreciate the unique perspectives and strengths that she brings to their lives, even amidst the occasional chaos and forgetfulness.

With Our Friends

Friendships are the lifeblood of our social existence, the threads that weave together the tapestry of our lives. They bring joy, laughter, and a sense of belonging. But what happens when the very fabric of our friendships is frayed by the challenges of ADHD? The impact can be profound, affecting not only us as individuals with ADHD but also those who stand by our side.

One of the most glaring hurdles is the difficulty of maintaining focus and engagement during conversations or social activities. Imagine being in the midst of a heartfelt discussion with a friend, only to find your mind wandering to a thousand different places. It's like trying to grasp a slippery fish, always slipping away just when you think you have it. The struggle to stay present and fully engaged often leaves us feeling disconnected and our friends wondering if they truly matter.

But it doesn't stop there. ADHD often brings with it an inconsistent follow-through on plans and commitments. It's not that we don't care about their friends or value their time together, far from it. It's the relentless nature of ADHD that plays tricks on memory and organization. Plans that were made with the best intentions can slip through the cracks, leaving our friends feeling frustrated and let down. The constant battle to stay on top of commitments can be exhausting, and the guilt that follows can weigh heavily on our hearts.

Forgetfulness and disorganization go hand in hand with ADHD, creating a perfect storm that can wreak havoc on friendships. And it's not that we don't want to be reliable or supportive; it's just that these minds are like a bustling marketplace, with thoughts and ideas swirling in a chaotic dance. The ability to keep track of important dates, events, and even simple tasks can be a monumental challenge. The result? Missed birthdays, forgotten coffee dates, and a sense of unreliability can strain even the strongest of friendships.

Emotional sensitivity and impulsivity add yet another layer of complexity to the ADHD friendship dynamic. The emotional rollercoaster that often accompanies ADHD can be intense and unpredictable. A seemingly harmless comment can be misconstrued, leading to hurt feelings and misunderstandings. Impulsivity can also rear its head, causing us to act on fleeting emotions without fully considering the consequences. These impulsive actions can leave our friends feeling bewildered and unsure of what to expect next.

So maybe you know a friend; you're reading this book, so you probably do, and you're wondering what you can do to help them and how you can learn to better relate to them. Well, here are a few things that you can try to do:

- **Educate yourself**: Empathy and understanding come when we will ourselves to open up our minds about those things that we do not understand. Learn about ADHD to better understand its challenges and how it affects your friend. This knowledge will help you approach situations with empathy and patience.

- **Be patient and understanding**: Recognize that these struggles with focus, organization, and impulsivity are not intentional. Be patient when plans change or commitments are forgotten, and offer understanding instead of frustration.

- **Communicate openly**: Maintain open lines of communication. Encourage them to share their thoughts and feelings about their ADHD and any challenges they may be facing. Be a good listener and offer a non-judgmental space for them to express themselves. You'd be surprised at just how much there is to learn.

- **Offer practical support**: There are small and big ways that you can make a difference. Help them stay organized by suggesting tools like calendars, reminders, or task lists. Offer to help with planning and keeping track of important dates or events. Small gestures can go a long way in easing their daily struggles.

- **Be flexible and adaptable**: Understand that their ADHD may lead to changes in plans or unexpected behaviors. Be flexible and adaptable, and try not to take these changes personally. Adaptability can help maintain a positive and supportive friendship.

- **Provide encouragement and positive reinforcement**: Celebrate with them their achievements, no matter how small. Offer words of encouragement and acknowledge their efforts. Positive reinforcement can boost their confidence and motivation.

- **Be a source of stability**: ADHD can bring a sense of chaos and unpredictability. Be a stable presence in your friend's life, offering consistency and reliability. Your friendship can provide a grounding force amidst the whirlwind of ADHD.

- **Avoid stigmatizing or labeling**: Refrain from stigmatizing or labeling based on their ADHD. Treat them as individuals, not defined solely by their condition. Focus on their strengths and unique qualities.

- **Encourage self-care**: Everybody needs to pour back into themselves. Remind them to prioritize self-care. Encourage them to engage in activities that help manage stress and promote well-being, such as exercise, hobbies, or mindfulness practices.

- **Offer non-judgmental support**: Finally, be that friend who feels like a safe landing place, a friend who listens without judgment. Create a safe space where your friend can openly discuss their challenges and emotions. Your support and understanding can make a significant impact on their well-being.

ADHD and Our Own Emotional Well-Being

This relationship that we have with ourselves is one of the most important that we will ever have. It shapes our emotional well-being, influences our self-esteem, and impacts our confidence. But when you have ADHD, this relationship can be a complex dance of frustration, shame, and self-blame.

Picture a stormy sea of emotions crashing against the shores of our minds. Living with ADHD can feel like being caught in the midst of this tempest, constantly battling against the waves. Frustration becomes a familiar companion as the challenges of staying organized, managing time, and completing tasks seem insurmountable. It's like trying to solve a puzzle with missing pieces, forever searching for that elusive sense of control. This frustration can morph into a heavy cloak of shame and self-blame, weighing down the spirit. Individuals with ADHD may question their abilities, feeling like they are constantly falling short of expectations. The whispers of self-doubt grow louder, eroding self-esteem and confidence.

But the emotional rollercoaster doesn't stop there. Regulating emotions and managing stress can be a Herculean task for those with ADHD. The impulsive nature of the condition can lead to outbursts or reactions that are as unpredictable as a lightning strike. Relationships can be strained, and a sense of guilt can settle in. The constant struggle to stay focused and organized can create a pressure cooker of stress, with deadlines looming and responsibilities piling up. It's like walking a tightrope, trying to maintain balance while the world spins around you. The weight of it all can leave individuals with ADHD feeling overwhelmed and emotionally drained.

In the midst of this storm, self-esteem and confidence can take a beating. The daily battles and setbacks can chip away at your sense of self-worth. It's easy to compare yourself to others who seem to effortlessly navigate life's challenges, further fueling feelings of inadequacy. This negative cycle can become a whirlpool, sucking away motivation and amplifying the difficulties of managing ADHD symptoms.

But we don't have to navigate these stormy weathers all on our own; friends, family, and loved ones can be the lighthouse in this stormy sea. By providing a safe harbor of understanding and empathy, they can help navigate the emotional challenges that ADHD presents. They can offer a listening ear without judgment, validating the struggles, and offering support. These people can become allies in developing coping strategies and stress management techniques, providing a helping hand when the load becomes too heavy to bear alone.

Fighting Against the Shame

In the battle against the shame that ADHD tries to inflict upon us, we must arm ourselves with compassion, understanding, and self-acceptance. It's time to rewrite the narrative and embrace our unique minds, turning our perceived weaknesses into strengths. Let's explore the strategies we can employ to fight back against shame and reclaim our self-worth.

First and foremost, we must cultivate self-compassion. Instead of bracing ourselves for the challenges that ADHD presents, let's offer kindness and understanding. Recognize that ADHD is not a character flaw or a personal failing but rather a neurological difference that shapes our experiences. Embrace the truth that we are doing the best we can with the tools we have, and that is something to be celebrated, not shamed.

Education is another powerful weapon in our arsenal. By learning about ADHD, we can gain a deeper understanding of its impact on our lives. Knowledge empowers us to challenge the misconceptions and stereotypes that society may impose upon us. Armed with accurate information, we can confidently advocate for ourselves and educate others, fostering a culture of empathy and acceptance.

Building a support network is crucial in our fight against shame. Surround ourselves with people who understand and uplift us, who see beyond the surface-level struggles, and who recognize our strengths. Seek out support groups, online communities, or therapy where we can connect with others who share similar experiences. Together, we can break the chains of shame and find solace in the understanding embrace of those who truly see us.

Shame often thrives in secrecy, so let's bring it into the light. Share our experiences with trusted friends, family members, or mental health professionals. Opening up about our struggles can be both liberating and empowering. It allows us to release the burden of shame and invites others to offer support and understanding.

Embracing our strengths and accomplishments is a vital aspect of combating shame. ADHD may present challenges, but it also gifts us with unique perspectives, creativity, and resilience. Celebrate our achievements, no matter how small they may seem. Recognize the progress we make each day and let go of the unrealistic expectations that shame tries to impose upon us.

Lastly, practicing self-acceptance is a powerful antidote to shame. Embrace our ADHD as an integral part of who we are rather than something to be ashamed of. Accept that our journey may be different from others, but that doesn't make it any less valuable or worthy. Embrace our quirks, our passions, and our unique way of navigating the world. By accepting ourselves fully, shame loses its grip, and we can step into our authentic selves with confidence and pride.

In this battle against shame, let us rise above the whispers of self-doubt and reclaim our self-worth. Let us stand together, united in our shared experiences, and refuse to let shame define us. With compassion, education, support, self-acceptance, and an unwavering belief in our own worth, we can conquer shame and embrace the beautiful tapestry of our ADHD-emboldened lives.

ADHD and Hormonal Changes

Hormonal changes are a natural part of a woman's life and have a profound impact on both her physical and mental well-being. When it comes to women with ADHD, hormonal fluctuations can exacerbate their existing symptoms, making the challenges they face even more pronounced. To truly grasp this impact, imagine a rollercoaster ride through a maze of emotions and cognitive shifts.

During monthly menstrual cycles, many women experience drastic shifts in hormone levels, particularly estrogen and progesterone. These hormonal fluctuations can contribute to the intensified symptoms of ADHD. Imagine feeling exhausted, dealing with painful cramps, and being overwhelmed by irritability on top of the usual struggles of ADHD. It's like battling through a storm while already navigating a tricky obstacle course.

Now, let's shift our focus to menopause, a phase of life when women experience a significant decline in hormone production. Hot flashes become a ubiquitous presence, robbing women of their comfort and disrupting their daily routines. These physical sensations are often accompanied by mood swings, adding a layer of emotional turbulence to an already challenging journey. For women with ADHD, this can mean facing even more pronounced difficulties in managing their attention, impulsiveness, and organization skills.

Consider, for a moment, the impact of these hormonal changes on cognitive functioning. ADHD symptoms such as forgetfulness, difficulty focusing, and disorganization can become intensified during hormonal fluctuations. Imagine trying to navigate a foggy labyrinth, with distractions pulling your attention in all directions and important details slipping through the cracks. It can feel like an uphill battle, both mentally and emotionally.

To further illustrate this concept, picture a tightrope walker trying to maintain balance while juggling multiple objects. Women with ADHD are already skilled jugglers but add hormonal changes into the mix, and it feels like the objects they're juggling become even heavier. It becomes a true test of resilience and adaptability.

While these challenges may feel overwhelming, there are various techniques and lifestyle adjustments that can significantly improve the overall well-being and symptom management of women with ADHD. Let's look at them.

- **Establish a Consistent Routine**: Implementing a structured daily routine can help minimize the impact of hormonal changes on ADHD symptoms. Set specific times for activities such as sleeping, eating, working, and leisure, as this can provide a sense of predictability and stability.

- **Prioritize Self-Care**: Taking care of your physical and emotional well-being is paramount during hormonal changes. Ensure that you are getting enough sleep, eating a balanced diet, and engaging in regular exercise. These practices can help stabilize mood, reduce fatigue, and improve cognitive functioning.

- **Cognitive Behavioral Therapy (CBT)**: Consider working with a therapist who specializes in CBT, as it can be highly effective in managing ADHD symptoms. CBT helps individuals recognize and challenge negative thought patterns, develop effective coping strategies, and improve time management and organization skills.

- **Medication and Alternative Treatments**: Consult with a healthcare professional who specializes in ADHD to explore medication options if necessary. Medications such as stimulants or non-stimulants can be prescribed to help manage symptoms. Additionally, some individuals find alternative treatments like mindfulness techniques, herbal supplements, or acupuncture helpful, though it's important to consult professionals before pursuing these options.

- **Stress Reduction Techniques**: Hormonal changes can increase stress levels, exacerbating ADHD symptoms. Engaging in stress reduction techniques such as deep breathing exercises, meditation, yoga, or engaging in hobbies can provide a sense of calm and improve focus and attention.

- **Support Network**: Surrounding yourself with a supportive network of family, friends, or support groups who understand your unique challenges can be immensely beneficial. Sharing experiences, seeking advice or validation, and receiving emotional support from others who can relate to your struggles can provide a sense of comfort and empowerment.

- **Environmental Modifications**: Creating an environment conducive to concentration and organization can greatly aid symptom management. Minimize distractions by organizing your physical space, using noise-cancelling headphones, or setting up designated work areas.

- **Time Management Strategies**: Many women with ADHD find it helpful to employ various time management techniques. Utilize tools such as timers, alarms, digital calendars, and to-do lists to stay organized and keep track of tasks and deadlines.

- **Regular Exercise**: Incorporating regular physical activity into your routine has been shown to improve mood, focus, and cognitive functioning. Engage in activities that you enjoy, such as walking, jogging, dancing, or joining group fitness classes.

- **Mindfulness and Relaxation Techniques**: Practicing mindfulness exercises and relaxation techniques can help reduce anxiety, improve focus, and enhance overall well-being. Activities such as deep breathing exercises, progressive muscle relaxation, guided imagery, or meditation can be incredibly beneficial.

Remember, managing the symptoms of ADHD during hormonal changes is a journey of self-discovery and finding what works best for you. Experiment with different strategies, be patient with yourself and seek support when needed. You have the power to navigate through these challenges with strength and resilience, finding balance and overall well-being along the way.

Chapter 2:

Building Self-Awareness

Have you ever sat and wondered what it means to accept yourself fully, like with all your ADHD quirks and shortcomings and all? In a world that often emphasizes conformity and expects us to fit into pre-defined molds, embracing our true selves can feel like a radical act of rebellion. But for women with ADHD, this journey of self-awareness and self-acceptance becomes even more profound and transformative. Imagine, for a moment, a tapestry woven with vibrant threads of unique personal traits, strengths, and challenges. This tapestry holds the essence of each woman's individuality, beautifully interwoven with the complexities of ADHD. It tells a powerful story of resilience, creativity, and limitless potential.

All too often, women with ADHD find themselves in a struggle for self-acceptance, battling against societal expectations and internalized criticism. They may have grown up feeling like square pegs trying to fit into round holes, constantly misunderstood, and plagued by feelings of inadequacy. The relentless inner voice whispers, "You're not good enough; you're broken; you should be like everyone else." But here's the truth: self-acceptance is the key that unlocks the door to empowerment, growth, and transformation. It is not about conforming or erasing those distinctive quirks and idiosyncrasies that make each woman with ADHD beautifully unique. Instead, it is about discovering, embracing, and celebrating those aspects of ourselves that set us apart.

In this second chapter of our journey together, we walk toward a path towards self-awareness and self-acceptance. We delve deep into the inner workings of the ADHD mind, unraveling its mysteries and shining a compassionate light on the struggles that have shaped us. We will navigate through the maze of emotions, successes, setbacks, and triumphs, exploring what it truly means to embrace ourselves wholeheartedly. Through this exploration, we will come to understand that self-acceptance is not a destination but a continuous journey. It requires patience, kindness, and unwavering self-compassion. It calls for the shedding of expectations and the embracing of imperfections. It invites us to redefine what it means to be successful and to acknowledge our own worthiness, regardless of society's measuring stick.

Together, we will peel back the layers of self-doubt, cultivating a fierce sense of self-love and resilience. We will learn to own our strengths, celebrate our accomplishments, and navigate through our challenges with grace and determination. In doing so, we will empower ourselves and others, redefining what it means to thrive in a world that often misunderstands and undervalues our unique brilliance.

So, are you ready to embark on this transformative journey? Open your heart, unleash your potential, and let the symphony of self-acceptance guide us as we weave a tapestry of authenticity, empowerment, and unapologetic self-love. Together, we will unravel the power of self-awareness and embark on a path towards embracing our ADHD identity with grace and unwavering acceptance.

Embracing Your Unique ADHD Traits

It's truly incredible when you decide to take ownership of your identity and who you are. The experience is transformative, like shedding an old skin to become your true self with confidence and self-assurance. When you know yourself and are comfortable in your own skin, you radiate energy that attracts positivity and opportunity into your life. You are more than your ADHD. You are the things that make you glow when you talk about them all; you are your passions and the things that set your soul on fire.

We're going to start this chapter off with an exercise because, honestly, I think that's the best place to start.

Step 1: Reflect on Your Personal Experiences (10 minutes)

Find a quiet and comfortable space where you can reflect without distractions. Take a few deep breaths, allowing yourself to settle into the present moment. Grab a pen and paper or open a new document on your computer. Think about your personal experiences with ADHD. Consider the challenges you have faced, the moments of triumph, and the lessons you have learned. Reflect on how ADHD has shaped your life, relationships, and aspirations. Jot down your thoughts, feelings, and memories as they come to you.

Step 2: Identify Your Unique Strengths (15 minutes)

Now, shift your focus to the strengths that accompany your ADHD. Every individual with ADHD possesses exceptional qualities that can be harnessed to achieve greatness. Here are some prompts to guide your exploration:

- **Hyperfocus**: Recall moments when you were deeply engrossed in an activity that captured your attention. What did you accomplish during those periods of intense focus? How did it make you feel?

- **Creativity**: Explore your imaginative side. How has ADHD fueled your creativity? Think about instances where your unique perspective led to innovative ideas or solutions.

- **Hyperactivity and Energy**: Consider the bursts of energy you experience. How have you channeled this energy into productive endeavors, hobbies, or physical activities? Reflect on the positive impact these moments have had on your life.

- **Intuition and Rapid Thinking**: Reflect on times when your quick thinking and ability to connect ideas rapidly allowed you to see patterns, solve problems, or make insightful decisions. How has this skill benefited you or others?

- **Resilience and Adaptability**: ADHD often requires adaptability and resilience. Recall moments when you successfully navigated through challenges, displaying your ability to bounce back and learn from setbacks.

Step 3: Embrace the Gift That Is Your ADHD (10 minutes)

Review the strengths you have identified and take a moment to truly embrace them. Recognize that these qualities are unique to you and can be incredible assets on your journey. Write down affirmations that celebrate your ADHD superpowers, such as:

- *My hyperfocus allows me to achieve exceptional results in my areas of passion.*

- *My creativity fuels my ability to think outside the box and find innovative solutions.*

- *My energy and enthusiasm bring joy and inspiration to those around me.*

- *My quick thinking and intuition help me make insightful decisions.*

- *My resilience and adaptability empower me to overcome obstacles and grow stronger.*

Step 4: Commit to Self-Acceptance and Empowerment (5 minutes)

As you conclude this exercise, make a commitment to yourself. Acknowledge that ADHD is an essential part of who you are, and it does not define your worth or potential. Embrace self-acceptance and empowerment. Repeat the following affirmation:

I am an extraordinary woman with ADHD. I embrace my unique strengths and use them to create a fulfilling and successful life. Today, I choose to celebrate the gifts of my ADHD. I choose to love all of who I am and all that I am.

There's no denying that ADHD can present obstacles in a world that values linear thinking and rigid structures. But what often seems to be forgotten is that it also endows you with a symphony of distinctive strengths: a vivid imagination, an unstoppable resilience, a striking ability to think outside the box, and the capacity to feel deeply, passionately, and exquisitely. You are not flawed; you are a vivid masterpiece in a world that is only just beginning to understand the depth of your hues.

ADHD is not a burden you carry; it is a part of what makes you, YOU. It is the flame that flickers and dances, refusing to be tamed and embodying the innate power that lies within you. It is the relentless spirit that propels you forward, the unquenchable curiosity that keeps you exploring, and the intense empathy that connects you to the world in a way few can comprehend.

Yes, there can be stormy days. Days when you feel like you're lost in a maze, running in circles. But remember, dear warrior, even the fiercest storms eventually yield to tranquility. It is in these storms that you find your strength, your grit, and your resolve. It is in these storms that you discover who you truly are.

Celebrate the untamed energy, the creative whirlwinds, the passionate outbursts, and the boundless zest for life that define the ADHD experience. Let us embrace the raw, beautiful chaos of our minds, for it is this chaos that births innovation, creativity, and progress.

Don't let the world tell you that you need to be *fixed*; you are not broken. You are different, and the difference is the mother of revolution. It is the catalyst for change. It is the spark that sets the world ablaze. Your traits are your secret weapons. Your ability to hyperfocus can help you master skills and dive deep into subjects that ignite your passion. Your innovative thinking can help you solve problems in ways others can't even imagine. Your sensitivity can make you a beacon of empathy, understanding, and connection in a world that desperately needs more of these qualities.

In your journey, reframe your ADHD not as a disorder but as a different order—a unique way of being that brings its own gifts and challenges. Look into the mirror and see not a woman with ADHD but a woman of power, a woman of resilience, a woman of extraordinary potential—a phoenix rising from the ashes, ready to set the world on fire.

How ADHD Contributes to Innovation and Creativity

- **Divergent thinking**: We excel at divergent thinking, which is the ability to generate multiple ideas and see connections between seemingly unrelated concepts. Their minds tend to make unique associations and think outside the box. This ability enables them to approach problems from unconventional angles and come up with innovative solutions.

- **Hyperfocus**: While ADHD is often associated with difficulties in maintaining focus, individuals with ADHD also experience periods of hyperfocus. Hyperfocus is an intense state of concentration and immersion in a particular task or activity. During these episodes, we often become fully absorbed, blocking out distractions and allowing our creativity to flow freely. This deep level of engagement can lead to breakthrough ideas and exceptional creative output.

- **Impulsivity**: Although impulsivity is generally considered a challenge in ADHD, it can also be a source of creative thinking. It makes us act on our ideas or make spontaneous decisions without overthinking, which can lead to novel approaches and unexpected solutions. Their willingness to take risks and explore uncharted territories can result in fresh perspectives and innovative outcomes.

- **Rapid idea generation**: ADHD individuals often have a stream of thoughts and ideas constantly flowing through their minds. This rapid idea generation can be a valuable asset in brainstorming sessions or creative endeavors. Their ability to generate a multitude of ideas quickly can enrich group discussions, inspire others, and contribute to a diverse range of possibilities.

- **Sensitivity and intuition**: Those of us with ADHD often have heightened sensitivity to their environment, emotions, and subtle cues. This heightened sensitivity can provide them with a deeper understanding of the world around them and the ability to perceive patterns and connections that others might overlook. They may have intuitive insights and make creative leaps based on these subtle perceptions.

- **Nonlinear thinking**: ADHD makes the mind work in nonlinear ways, making unexpected connections and leaps in thinking. This nonlinear thinking style can lead to innovative ideas and unconventional problem-solving approaches. It makes you see patterns, possibilities, and solutions that others might miss due to their more linear thinking patterns.

Confronting Guilt, Shame, and Stigma

Shame and guilt can be significant and complex emotional experiences when you're living with ADHD. Exploring the concept of shame in the context of ADHD can provide valuable insights into its origins and effects.

Shame, at its core, is a deeply ingrained feeling of unworthiness or inadequacy. It arises when we perceive a discrepancy between our own self-perceived shortcomings and societal or personal expectations. For us, that shame often emerges from the challenges and unique characteristics associated with the condition.

One of the key factors contributing to our shame about ADHD is the pervasive sense of underachievement. We struggle with organization, time management, and focusing on tasks, leading to difficulties in meeting expectations at home, work, or in relationships. Persistent patterns of forgetfulness, impulsivity, and distractibility can evoke feelings of incompetence and failure, triggering shame.

ADHD-related symptoms also frequently manifest in social and interpersonal contexts. Women with ADHD may experience difficulties with active listening, maintaining attention during conversations, and regulating impulsive reactions. These challenges can lead to misunderstandings, strained communication, and feelings of guilt or embarrassment, intensifying their experience of shame in relationships.

The societal misconceptions and stereotypes surrounding ADHD also contribute to the shame we experience. ADHD is often associated with hyperactive and disruptive behavior, primarily observed in boys during childhood. We start to internalize feelings of being different, flawed, or abnormal. We feel this pressure to camouflage our symptoms, leading to a constant fear of being exposed or judged, which fuels shame.

Shame, when left unaddressed, can have detrimental effects on our mental health and relationships. It can lead to feelings of isolation, low self-esteem, and a reluctance to seek support or disclose one's struggles. Shame can hinder the development of healthy relationships by fostering a fear of vulnerability and intimacy.

To holistically explore shame in ADHD women, it is important to consider both individual and societal perspectives. By promoting awareness, education, and destigmatizing ADHD, society can help reduce the shame experienced by women with the condition. Additionally, therapeutic interventions that focus on self-compassion, acceptance, and building coping strategies can empower individuals to challenge shame and develop healthier relationship dynamics.

By delving into the concept of shame and its relationship with ADHD in women, your book can provide valuable insights and guidance for both individuals with ADHD and those who interact with them. Understanding the complexities of shame can foster empathy and support and ultimately contribute to building more inclusive and understanding relationships.

Unpacking and learning to deal with the shame and the guilt

Through unpacking and challenging our shame, we can reclaim our power and embrace our unique strengths.

Rise and reshape the narrative. Just like the mythical bird (the phoenix) that rises from the ashes, we too, have the power to transform our shame into strength. Instead of allowing shame to define us, we can choose to see it as an opportunity for growth. By reframing our experiences and recognizing that ADHD is not a personal failing but a neurological difference, we can rise above shame and embrace our individuality. We get to define and determine our own identity. Not the other way around.

Embrace the kaleidoscope. Instead of feeling ashamed of your scattered thoughts and hyperactivity, you can celebrate the unique way our minds work. Reframing ADHD as a superpower rather than a limitation can help unlock your creativity, intuition, and resilience.

Make space for and enjoy your journey. Just like a butterfly undergoes a transformative journey, we, too, can embrace our own metamorphosis. Rather than hiding in shame, we can embrace our struggles as stepping stones towards personal growth. We can emerge from our cocoons as empowered individuals who refuse to be defined by shame.

Piece through the puzzle of self-acceptance. Your journey to self-acceptance is like a puzzle, with each piece representing a different aspect of your ADHD experience. As women with ADHD, we can challenge shame by gradually piecing together our strengths, accomplishments, and unique qualities. Focusing on what makes us exceptional rather than dwelling on perceived shortcomings creates a complete picture of self-acceptance.

Nurturing Positive Relationships

Imagine, if you will, the tender petals of a budding flower delicately nurtured by the warm embrace of sunlight and nourishing rain. This image right here is what reflects the essence of a healthy relationship for a woman with ADHD. Like the flower, you too, require an environment that fosters growth, acceptance, and compassion.

A nurturing relationship begins with an unwavering foundation of empathy. It is a sanctuary where your quirks, your unfiltered thoughts, and your restless spirit find solace. Your partner, with an empathetic touch, understands that your mind is a kaleidoscope of ideas, forever in motion and never confined to a linear path. In this sanctuary, you are free to explore her boundless potential without fear of judgment or rejection.

Imagine a gentle breeze on a balmy summer evening, caressing your skin and whispering sweet nothings in your ear. This is what understanding feels like in the context of your relationships. It is a symphony of patience and acceptance, where your people take the time to truly comprehend the intricacies of your mind. They recognize that your forgetfulness is not a sign of carelessness but rather a manifestation of your vibrant imagination. With understanding, her partner becomes her compass, guiding her through the labyrinth of distractions and helping her find her way back to focus.

Yet the most profound aspect of a nurturing relationship lies in the unwavering support that blossoms within its embrace. Imagine a towering oak tree, why don't you? Its roots are firmly planted in the earth, providing shelter and strength to all who seek refuge beneath its branches. Similarly, we thrive when we find and have those people who become our steadfast pillars, providing stability and encouragement.

In this sanctuary of love, connections become our advocates, championing our dreams and aspirations. They recognize your unique strengths and talents, even when you struggle to see them yourself. They celebrate your victories, no matter how small, and gently remind her that setbacks are merely stepping stones on the path to growth. With unwavering support, they empower you to embrace your ADHD as a gift rather than a burden.

Tips for Nurturing Positive Relationships

As women with ADHD, we possess a unique and vibrant spirit that has the power to ignite and enrich the relationships we hold dear. Look at some of the ways in which we can nurture and cultivate positive connections, ensuring that the heartstrings of our relationships resonate with love, understanding, and unwavering support.

First and foremost, nurturing positive relationships begins with self-awareness and self-acceptance. We must embrace the beautiful chaos that resides within us, acknowledging our strengths and weaknesses, quirks, and idiosyncrasies. By understanding ourselves on a deeper level, we can effectively communicate our needs to our partners, friends, and loved ones. When we are open and honest about our

ADHD, we invite them to join us on this journey, fostering a foundation of empathy and understanding.

Communication, like a gentle breeze, carries the seeds of understanding and strengthens the roots of our relationships. As women with ADHD, we may find it challenging to articulate our thoughts and feelings at times. However, by practicing active listening and expressing ourselves with clarity and patience, we can bridge the gap between our minds and the hearts of those we hold dear. Let us remember that communication is a two-way street. We must also encourage our loved ones to share their thoughts and emotions, creating an environment of reciprocal understanding and support.

Boundaries, like protective walls, are essential for nurturing positive relationships. As women with ADHD, we may feel overwhelmed and easily distracted, leading to a sense of chaos in our lives. By setting boundaries, we safeguard our mental and emotional well-being, enabling us to be fully present in our relationships. Communicate your needs openly and honestly, allowing your loved ones to support you in maintaining those boundaries. Remember, boundaries are not a sign of weakness but rather a testament to self-care and self-respect.

In the garden of relationships, patience, and forgiveness bloom like delicate flowers, adding beauty and resilience to our connections. As women with ADHD, we may stumble, forget, or become easily distracted. It is crucial to cultivate patience within ourselves and extend that grace to our loved ones. Embrace the understanding that mistakes and missteps are part of the journey, and forgiveness is the fertile soil that allows relationships to grow and flourish.

Finally, the most profound way to nurture positive relationships is to celebrate and cherish the unique strengths and talents of both ourselves and our loved ones. Recognize that ADHD brings with it a myriad of gifts, such as creativity, resilience, and the ability to think outside the box. By embracing these strengths and encouraging them in our loved ones, we build a foundation of support and empowerment that allows us all to thrive.

Techniques for Effectively Expressing ADHD-Related Needs and Challenges to Loved Ones

There's an expression that I really love, and it says: Closed mouths don't get fed. This is enlightening, as it is a sobering truth to take in.

In the realm of relationships, the importance of effective communication cannot be overstated. This holds especially true for those of us with ADHD, who often face unique difficulties in articulating their needs and challenges. Recognizing and voicing these struggles is crucial not only for personal growth and self-advocacy but also for fostering understanding and empathy within their relationships.

This expression again, "closed, mouths don't get fed" is a powerful reminder of the necessity to speak up about our ADHD-related experiences. Keeping our struggles hidden and internalized can lead to feelings of isolation, frustration, and, in some cases, even resentment. When we choose to embrace vulnerability and voice our needs, we open the door to potential solutions, understanding, and support from our loved ones.

With that in mind, let's explore some techniques that can assist individuals with ADHD in effectively expressing their needs and challenges within their relationships.

Now, let's look at a few techniques you can look at to help you improve your communication:

- **Educate yourself and your partner**: Knowledge is power, and this rings especially true when it comes to ADHD. Take the time to research and learn about your condition and its impact on your daily life. Share this knowledge with your partner, helping them understand the unique challenges you face. Encourage open and honest conversations about ADHD, promoting a shared understanding and empathy.

- **Choose the right time and place**: Timing is everything when discussing sensitive topics. Find a calm and relaxed environment where both you and your partner can fully engage in the conversation. Avoid discussing important matters when either of you is already stressed, tired, or overwhelmed, as it can hinder effective communication.

- **Use those "I" statements**: When expressing your needs or challenges, using "I" statements can be tremendously helpful. This approach focuses on your personal experiences and emotions rather than blaming or accusing your partner. For example, instead of saying, "You never listen to me," try saying, "I feel unheard when I'm interrupted during our conversations."

- **Active listening**: Communication is a two-way street. Encourage your partner to actively listen and validate your experiences. Similarly, make a conscious effort to actively listen to their perspective. This promotes a healthy dialogue, allowing both parties to feel heard and understood.

- **Explore verbal communication tools**: Words may not always effectively convey your thoughts and emotions, especially for those with ADHD who may struggle with verbal expression. Consider incorporating non-verbal communication tools such as writing letters, using visual aids like charts or diagrams, or even utilizing artistic outlets to express yourself more effectively.

Remember, effective communication is a continuous process that requires patience, understanding, and practice. By consciously choosing to work on our struggles and addressing them accordingly, we can increase our ability to express our needs and challenges, leading to stronger, more fulfilling relationships.

x

Promoting Empathy and Understanding Among Family, Friends, and Partners

Empathy, a tapestry woven with threads of compassion and understanding, is a profound connection that binds us all. It is the gentle touch that mends broken hearts and the soothing voice that whispers solace in times of despair. Like a mirror reflecting the depths of another's soul, empathy allows us to step into the shoes of another and feel their joys and sorrows as if they were our own.

In this chaotic world, empathy becomes the bridge that unites us, transcending the boundaries of race, religion, and culture. It is a beacon of light that illuminates the darkest corners of human suffering, reminding us that we are not alone in our struggles. Through empathy, we become not only witnesses but active participants in the lives of others, embracing their pain and offering solace, their triumphs, and celebrating alongside them.

Empathy is a testament to our shared humanity in a world that frequently suffers from indifference and apathy. It is the catalyst for change, the catalyst for understanding and acceptance. Empathy allows us to see beyond our own narrow perspectives, embrace the diversity that colors our world, and cultivate a genuine sense of compassion for those who walk different paths.

Empathy is important because it breathes life into our relationships, fostering deeper connections and nurturing bonds that withstand the test of time. It is a gentle reminder that we are all fragile beings seeking love, validation, and understanding. Through empathy, we create a safe space for vulnerability, where masks can be shed, and authentic connections can flourish. It also has the power to heal wounds, both seen and unseen. It holds the potential to mend the broken fragments of society and bridge the gaps that divide us. It allows us to break free from the chains of judgment and prejudice, embrace the beauty of diversity, and build a world where kindness and compassion are the cornerstones of our interactions.

Lastly, I want to say that it is the vibrant thread that weaves us together, reminding us that our stories are intertwined. It opens our hearts and minds, cultivating a deeper understanding of the human condition. With empathy, we can create a world where listening is valued over speaking, where understanding triumphs over ignorance, and where compassion becomes the guiding force in our interactions.

Placing empathy within our friends and family circles is necessary if we want to feel not so alone in our struggles. Here is a list of suggestions on some of the ways in which we can work on building empathy with our friends and family:

- **Share your experiences**: One of the most effective ways to build empathy is through personal storytelling. Share your own experiences with ADHD, highlighting the challenges you face, how it impacts your daily life, and the strategies you use to manage it. By providing this window into your world, you allow your friends and family to gain insight and a deeper understanding of what you go through.

- **Educate them on ADHD**: Empathy flourishes when there is knowledge and understanding. Provide educational resources, articles, and books about ADHD that highlight the unique experiences of women with the condition. Encourage your loved ones to learn about the cognitive and emotional differences associated with ADHD, helping them grasp the intricacies of your world.

- **Open communication channels**: Create a safe and non-judgmental space for open conversation. Encourage your friends and family to ask questions and voice their curiosity about ADHD. Foster an environment where they feel comfortable seeking clarification and understanding. Utilize active listening techniques to ensure their perspectives are also heard and validated.

- **Engage in perspective-taking exercises**: To truly understand the challenges faced by individuals with ADHD, it can be beneficial for friends and family to engage in perspective-taking exercises. Encourage them to reflect on situations where they may have experienced similar difficulties or faced unique hurdles. This exercise can help foster empathy by making them more attuned to the struggles of others.

- **Foster a supportive network**: Surrounding yourself with a supportive network is crucial for individuals with ADHD.

Encourage your friends and family to be part of this support system by attending therapy sessions, joining support groups, or participating in workshops related to ADHD. This not only helps them understand the condition better but also empowers them to offer informed and compassionate support.

- **Encourage self-reflection**: Empathy begins with self-awareness. Encourage your friends and family to reflect on their own biases, assumptions, and judgments. Help them understand that ADHD is a neurological condition, not a personal failing and that offering support and understanding is essential to fostering healthy relationships.

Unleashing Your Potential

Just because you have ADHD does not mean that you can't set goals for yourself or consistently challenge yourself to become the very best version of yourself. You are limitless, so go out there and conquer the world because the only person who can give you the kind of life you are looking for is YOU. But first, there are a few key things that you should focus on. These are:

- **Focus and Direction**: Setting clear goals provides individuals with ADHD with a sense of focus and direction. With ADHD often characterized by distractibility and difficulty maintaining attention, having well-defined goals can serve as a compass, guiding their efforts and keeping them on track.

- **Motivation and Engagement**: Goals act as catalysts for motivation. By setting meaningful and achievable goals, you can tap into your intrinsic motivation, driving you to overcome challenges and stay engaged in your tasks. Goals provide a sense of purpose, making it easier to stay motivated and committed.

- **Organization and Prioritization**: ADHD can make it challenging to prioritize and organize tasks effectively. However, goal setting can help individuals with ADHD break down larger objectives into smaller, manageable steps. This allows for better organization and prioritization, making it easier to tackle tasks one at a time, reducing overwhelm, and increasing productivity.

- **Time Management**: Time management can be a struggle, often leading to procrastination or feeling overwhelmed by deadlines. Setting specific goals with clear timelines helps develop strategies to manage time more effectively. Breaking down goals into smaller, time-bound tasks creates a structured framework and promotes a sense of accountability.

- **Self-Awareness and Reflection**: Goal setting encourages individuals with ADHD to reflect on their strengths, weaknesses, and areas for growth. By setting goals that align with their interests and abilities, individuals can gain a deeper understanding of themselves and their potential. Regularly reflecting on progress and adjusting goals accordingly fosters self-awareness and personal growth.

- **Celebrating Achievements**: Goal setting allows you to celebrate accomplishments, no matter how small. Recognizing progress and celebrating milestones boosts self-confidence and reinforces positive behaviors. This positive reinforcement creates a cycle of motivation and encourages individuals to continue striving for their goals.

- **Building Resilience**: You may face setbacks and obstacles along your journey. However, goal setting helps develop resilience by teaching you to persevere, adapt, and problem-solve when faced with challenges. By setting realistic goals and learning from setbacks, individuals with ADHD can build resilience and cultivate a growth mindset.

That's the end of this chapter. In the next one, we tackle all things related to communicating well, even with ADHD, because, as you might already know, relationships blossom when we make effective communication the heart and center of our interactions.

Chapter 3:

Communicating With Partners

Amanda sat at the kitchen table, feeling overwhelmed and frustrated. She had been diagnosed with ADHD a while ago, and while she had made progress in managing her symptoms, one area that continued to challenge her was communication with her partner, Eric. Despite their deep love for each other, Amanda often struggled to express her thoughts and emotions in a way that Eric could understand. On this particular evening, Amanda's frustration had reached its peak. She had been trying to explain her need for more emotional support, only to be met with confused looks and unintentional dismissiveness from Eric. It seemed as though they were speaking entirely different languages despite sharing the same space and the same love.

As tears welled up in her eyes, Amanda remembered a piece of advice she had received from her therapist. "Communication is a dance," the therapist had said. "Creating a beautiful routine takes two partners moving in harmony."

Determined to find a way to break the communication barrier with Eric, Amanda decided to approach the situation differently. She knew that simply telling him what she needed wasn't enough; she had to show him.

The next day, as Eric sat in his favorite armchair, engrossed in a book, Amanda approached him with a mischievous smile. She held up a blindfold and said, "Close your eyes and trust me."

Curiosity piqued, and Eric closed his eyes, not knowing what was about to happen. Amanda gently guided him to his feet and led him to the center of the living room. With the blindfold securely in place, Eric stood there, slightly nervous but intrigued.

Amanda's heart pounded with anticipation. She had carefully planned each step of the dance, wanting to create a physical representation of their communication struggles. With a soft melody playing in the background, she took Eric's hands in hers and began to move.

Their dance started out chaotic, with Amanda intentionally leading Eric in a series of abrupt, disjointed movements. It symbolized the frustration and confusion that often dominated their conversations. But then, as the music shifted, Amanda changed her approach.

Guiding Eric into a graceful waltz, Amanda demonstrated the power of clear and empathetic communication. Every step she took was deliberate, mirroring the way she wanted their conversations to flow. She listened attentively, validating Eric's emotions and responding thoughtfully. It was a dance of understanding, a language spoken without words.

As the dance came to an end, Amanda removed Eric's blindfold. He looked at her, his eyes filled with a mix of awe and realization. At that moment, he understood the significance of what they had just experienced.

From that day forward, Amanda and Eric made a conscious effort to communicate with each other in a way that honored their dance. They recognized that it took patience, vulnerability, and a willingness to truly listen to one another. Their relationship blossomed as they learned to move together, harmonizing their thoughts and feelings in perfect synchronization.

Through the power of dance, Amanda and Eric discovered that communication was not just about words but about understanding, empathy, and connection. It was a beautiful reminder that sometimes the most profound conversations happen when we let our bodies speak the language of the heart.

Communication Challenges

In a world that often expects women to effortlessly juggle multiple roles and responsibilities, those with ADHD face unique and often overlooked communication challenges. Imagine stepping into the vibrant life of a woman; we'll call her Emily, a young woman with ADHD, as she navigates a typical day, encountering the hurdles that arise from her condition.

As Emily enters her bustling workplace, she finds herself surrounded by a cacophony of voices, phones ringing, and the constant hum of activity. For her, this seemingly ordinary environment can quickly become overwhelming. ADHD makes it difficult for her to filter out distractions and focus on the task at hand. As a result, she struggles to maintain clear and concise communication amidst the chaos.

During a team meeting, Emily's mind races, trying to capture every detail discussed. However, her ADHD often causes her to lose track of her thoughts, leading to frequent interruptions or unfinished sentences. As she stumbles over her words, she can feel the weight of the judgmental gazes from her colleagues. It's not that she lacks intelligence or insights; her mind simply works in a way that doesn't conform to the traditional communication norms.

Outside of the workplace, Emily yearns for deep connections and meaningful conversations. However, her ADHD can interfere with her ability to engage in sustained dialogues. She might find herself interrupting friends or losing focus mid-conversation, unintentionally derailing the flow. It's not that she doesn't value the interaction—it's just that her mind is a whirlwind of thoughts, constantly vying for attention.

In her romantic relationships, Emily encounters additional communication challenges. When discussing sensitive topics, her ADHD can amplify emotional responses, leading to impulsive reactions and misunderstandings. It's as if her emotions are heightened, swirling within her like a tempest. Expressing herself in a calm and collected manner becomes an arduous task, leaving her feeling frustrated and unheard.

Amidst these struggles, Emily knows that she possesses immense strengths as well. Her ADHD grants her a unique perspective on the world—a vibrant tapestry of creativity, spontaneity, and ingenuity. Despite the communication hurdles she faces, she remains resilient and determined to find ways to bridge the gap between her mind and the world around her.

Emily discovers that creating structure and incorporating visual aids into her communication can be game-changers. Color-coded calendars, to-do lists, and even sketches become her trusted allies in conveying her thoughts effectively. She also learns to advocate for herself, openly discussing her ADHD with her loved ones and colleagues, fostering understanding and empathy. Like Emily, we too can learn to navigate these communication challenges and ensure that we build healthier and stronger relationships with those who are closest to us.

Managing ADHD Symptoms During Communication

Impulsivity in communication is like riding a rollercoaster blindfolded. One minute, you're sharing your favorite childhood memories, and the next, you're sharing your deepest secrets with the barista at your local coffee shop. It's a whirlwind of words and emotions, leaving you wondering how you ended up on this wild ride. So, what can you do to better learn to navigate these spontaneous conversational waters?

- **"Think before you speak" becomes "Think while you speak but speak anyway!"** We all know that thinking before speaking is easier said than done. Embrace your unique thought process and give yourself permission to express your ideas, even if they come out a little differently than planned.

- **"Pause Button" Technique**: When you feel the urge to blurt out the first thing that comes to mind, imagine there's a magical pause button right in front of you. Take a moment, press it, and allow yourself to consider the consequences before hitting play.

- **"Three-second Rule:"** Count to three in your head before responding to someone. This brief pause can help you gather your thoughts and respond more thoughtfully, reducing the chances of impulsive outbursts or misunderstandings.

- **Embrace the art of "Awkward Silence"**: Sometimes, silence can be golden. Embrace those awkward pauses in conversation as opportunities to reflect, gather your thoughts, and respond in a way that truly represents your intentions.

- **Channel your inner "Detective:"** Before jumping to conclusions or responding impulsively, take a moment to gather additional information. Ask questions, clarify misunderstandings, and uncover the full picture before forming your response.

- **The power of "I'll get back to you:"** It's okay not to have all the answers immediately. Give yourself permission to say, "I'll get back to you on that," allowing yourself time to gather your thoughts and respond more effectively.

- **GIF Game**: Use humor to diffuse potentially impulsive situations. Keep a collection of funny GIFs or memes on hand to add a touch of levity to conversations, lightening the mood and giving yourself a moment to regroup.

- **Find your "Communication Wingman:"** Get that trusted friend or loved one who understands your communication challenges. Have them serve as your "wingman," helping you navigate conversations, offering reminders, and providing feedback when needed.

Forgetfulness and Disorganization

The funniest thing to ever happen to me due to forgetfulness and disorganization in communication was when I confidently walked into a meeting, only to realize I had forgotten my notes, my agenda, and even my own name. It was like stepping into a comedy sketch but without the canned laughter. If you've ever found yourself in a similar situation, here are some useful tips to help you conquer that forgetfulness.

- **The Sticky Note Army**: Embrace the power of sticky notes! Cover your workspace with colorful reminders, to-do lists, and important details. Not only will they catch your attention, but they'll also add a vibrant touch to your environment.

- **Phone Alarm Symphony**: Set multiple alarms on your phone to remind you of important meetings, deadlines, and even simple tasks. Let the sweet sound of your phone's alarm become your personal orchestra, conducting your day with precision.

- **Befriended Calendar:** Make friends with your calendar app or a trusty physical planner. Use it religiously to jot down appointments, deadlines, and even personal reminders. Let it be your reliable sidekick in the battle against forgetfulness.

- **Power of Repetition**: Repeat important information to yourself out loud. Whether it's someone's name, a meeting time, or a grocery list, saying it multiple times helps solidify it in your memory. Just be careful not to do it in public, or you might get some amusing looks!

- **Backup Plan Brigade**: Always have a backup plan in place. If you're notorious for forgetting key points in a conversation, jot them down on a small notepad or use a voice recorder app on your phone. These backups will be your secret weapons when memory fails you.

- **Delegate Dance:** Don't be afraid to delegate tasks and responsibilities to others when possible. Whether it's asking a colleague to remind you of important dates or getting a family member to help you stay organized, teamwork can make the forgetfulness dream work!

- **Art of Laughter**: Embrace the humor in your forgetfulness and disorganization. Laugh at yourself when you misplace your keys for the hundredth time or forget what you were saying mid-sentence. Laughter not only lightens the mood, but it also helps you bounce back and move forward.

- **Forgiveness Factor**: Finally, forgive yourself for the occasional forgetful blunders. We're all humans, and ADHD brings its own unique challenges. Remember that mistakes happen, and it's how we learn and grow from them that truly matters.

Minimizing Distractions During Important Conversations

The thing about being easily distracted is that it's like trying to have a focused conversation while surrounded by a marching band, fireworks, and a parade of adorable puppies. It's a constant battle to keep our attention on track and avoid veering off into the land of shiny distractions. So, what do you do? What do you do to prevent and protect yourself from getting lost in all that craziness?

- **The Zen Zone**: Find a quiet and clutter-free space for important conversations. Create your own little oasis of calm where distractions are minimized, allowing you to focus your attention on the conversation at hand.

- **Art of Eye Contact**: Maintain eye contact with the person you're speaking with. Not only does this show respect and engagement, but it also helps keep you anchored in the conversation, preventing your mind from wandering off to that mental grocery list.

- **The Silencing Symphony**: Put your phone on silent mode or, better yet, keep it out of sight. Those notifications can wait! By silencing the constant pings and vibrations, you'll create a distraction-free zone and give your full attention to the conversation.

- **The Power of Listening**: Practice active listening techniques, such as nodding, summarizing, and asking clarifying questions. Engaging in the conversation actively will help keep your mind focused and prevent it from wandering off to that YouTube video of cats playing the piano.

- **The Pomodoro Technique**: Break important conversations into smaller, manageable chunks. Set a timer for focused conversation intervals, followed by short breaks. This structured approach can help keep your attention from drifting and improve overall engagement.

- **The Fascinating Fidgets**: Keep a small, discreet fidget toy or object in your pocket. Something you can discreetly manipulate with your hands during a conversation. This can help redirect restless energy and keep you more present in the moment.

- **The Self-Talk Show**: Use self-talk to consciously remind yourself to stay focused. Mentally repeat phrases like "stay present" or "listen attentively" as gentle reminders to keep your mind from wandering off to that mental image of a llama wearing sunglasses.

- **The Accountability Ally**: Enlist the help of a trusted friend or family member to hold you accountable for staying focused during important conversations. Ask them to gently remind you to refocus if they notice your attention starting to drift.

Time Management Techniques for Better Communication

Did you actually know that better time management could make you a better communicator? Yup, that's right! Time management isn't just about ticking off items on a to-do list or squeezing more tasks into your day. It can actually enhance your communication skills and make you a more effective and efficient communicator.

- **Prioritization**: Start by identifying your most important communication tasks. Prioritize them based on urgency and importance. By tackling high-priority items first, you'll ensure that your crucial messages are delivered promptly and effectively.

- **Calendar magic**: Utilize your calendar as a powerful tool for scheduling communication-related activities. Block out dedicated time slots for important conversations, emails, or phone calls. This way, you'll have designated periods solely devoted to effective communication.

- **Inbox Intervention**: Take control of your email inbox! Implement strategies like setting specific times to check and respond to emails, utilizing filters and folders to organize messages, and unsubscribing from unnecessary newsletters. A decluttered inbox means less time wasted and more focus on meaningful communication.

- **Power of Brevity**: Embrace the art of concise communication. Aim to be clear, direct, and to the point. Avoid unnecessary rambling or excessive details that can dilute your message. Remember, brevity is not only the soul of wit but also the key to effective communication.

- **Meeting Makeover**: Transform your meetings by making them more efficient and productive. Set clear agendas, establish time limits for each topic, and encourage active participation. By keeping meetings focused and streamlined, you'll maximize communication impact while minimizing time wastage.

- **The Magic of Active Listening**: Practice active listening techniques to enhance your communication skills. Give your full attention, maintain eye contact, and provide verbal and non-verbal cues to show engagement. Being an active listener not only improves understanding but also saves time by avoiding misunderstandings and unnecessary repetitions.

- **The Power of "No"**: Learn to say no when necessary. Overcommitting yourself can lead to overwhelm and poor communication. Prioritize your time and energy, and politely decline requests that don't align with your priorities or availability. By setting boundaries, you'll have more focused time for meaningful communication.

- **Time-Out Technique:** Take regular breaks to recharge and rejuvenate. Stepping away from work allows you to return with a fresh perspective and renewed energy. These breaks can also serve as opportunities for informal communication and relationship-building with colleagues or loved ones.

Non-Verbal Communication

In communication, the words said are just as important as the ones not said, believe it or not. And when it comes to nonverbal cues—those unspoken messages that dance through the air—ADHD can sometimes throw a curveball into the mix. It's like trying to solve a puzzle while someone keeps rearranging the pieces just for fun.

Our ADHD brains have a knack for hyperfocusing on the verbal fireworks—the words that explode in conversation. We're like magpies, drawn to shiny objects of speech. But amidst this linguistic extravaganza, we may miss the silent fireworks happening around us. Those subtle nonverbal cues that others seem to effortlessly pick up on, like a secret language of the unspoken.

Imagine you're in a conversation, and as you're enthusiastically sharing your latest adventure, your friend raises an eyebrow ever so slightly. Ah, the raised eyebrow, a nonverbal cue that signals skepticism or curiosity. But alas, your ADHD brain, caught up in the whirlwind of words, fails to catch this fleeting expression. You continue your tale, blissfully unaware of the silent question mark hanging in the air.

Or perhaps you're at a party, surrounded by a sea of mingling people. As you navigate through the crowd, you notice a group engaged in animated conversation. Their body postures lean forward, their eyes locked in an unspoken dance of connection. Ah, the dance of engagement, a nonverbal cue that speaks volumes. But your ADHD radar, ever attuned to the verbal symphony, fails to pick up on this subtle choreography. You approach the group, unaware of the invisible force field that signals their closed circle.

Understanding nonverbal cues doesn't have to feel like an insurmountable task. You just need that dash of awareness and knowledge around all those different types of non-verbal cues.

First, we have facial expressions, those telltale signs that paint emotions on our canvas of communication. A smile can indicate happiness, while a furrowed brow might suggest confusion or concern. So, when someone flashes a smile like a ray of sunshine, bask in its warmth and respond accordingly.

Next, we have eye contact, the window to the soul. Maintaining eye contact shows attentiveness and interest, while avoiding it may signal shyness or discomfort. So, lock eyes like a master detective, but remember to blink occasionally to avoid creeping people out.

Gestures—how they speak volumes without uttering a word. A thumbs-up can convey approval, while a finger to the lips indicates the need for silence. So, give a thumbs-up when your friend nails that high note in karaoke, but save the finger to the lips for when you want to shush that talkative parrot in the corner.

Ah, body posture, the silent language of our physical selves. Leaning forward can demonstrate engagement, while crossed arms might imply defensiveness or disagreement. So, lean in like a curious cat when someone shares their passions, but be cautious of crossing your arms like a fortress wall, lest you unintentionally shut down the conversation.

Proxemics, which is the art of personal space. Standing close to someone can indicate intimacy or familiarity, while keeping a distance may suggest a need for personal space. So, respect the invisible bubble around others unless you're their best friend or a professional bubble burster.

Touch is the gentle language of connection. A warm handshake can convey friendliness, while a pat on the back can express encouragement. So, shake hands like a politician on the campaign trail, but save the back pat for when your friend conquers that fear of spiders.

The tone of voice, the melodic symphony of communication. A soft tone can convey sensitivity, while a loud tone might indicate excitement or anger. So, modulate your voice like a seasoned actor, but beware of accidentally shouting your grocery list in the cereal aisle.

Clothing and appearance are the visual cues that set the stage. Formal attire can suggest professionalism, while casual clothing may imply a relaxed environment. So, dress the part like a chameleon, adapting to the social context without losing your unique style.

And finally, microexpressions—those split-second flashes of emotion that reveal our true feelings. A fleeting smile, a subtle frown, a quick raise of an eyebrow. These microexpressions are like the hidden treasures of nonverbal communication, waiting to be discovered by the keen observer. Here are a couple more microexpressions that would be beneficial to pay attention to:

- **Surprise**: A split-second widening of the eyes and raised eyebrows, often accompanied by a slight drop of the jaw. For example, when someone receives unexpected news or sees something astonishing.

- **Disgust:** A subtle wrinkling of the nose and upper lip, sometimes accompanied by a slight narrowing of the eyes. This expression can be seen when someone encounters something unpleasant or offensive.

- **Contempt**: A slight curling of the lip on one side, indicating a sense of superiority or disdain towards someone or something.

- **Fear:** Wide eyes, raised eyebrows, and a slightly open mouth. This expression is often seen in response to a perceived threat or danger.

- **Anger**: A tightening of the jaw, narrowed eyes, and furrowed brows. This microexpression signifies frustration, irritation, or anger.

- **Sadness**: A downward turn of the mouth, drooping eyebrows, and a slight narrowing of the eyes. This expression reflects feelings of sorrow, grief, or disappointment.

- **Happiness**: A quick upward movement of the corners of the mouth, sometimes accompanied by crinkling around the eyes. This microexpression conveys joy, contentment, or amusement.

- **Confusion**: A slight furrowing of the brow and a quizzical expression. This microexpression indicates uncertainty or a lack of understanding.

- **Contemplation**: A thoughtful expression with a slight tilt of the head, indicating deep thinking or reflection.

Remember, microexpressions are fleeting and can be challenging to spot. Paying attention to these subtle cues can help you better understand the emotions and intentions of those around you. But it's also important to consider context and other nonverbal cues to get a more accurate interpretation. Happy decoding!

Ways to Increase Your Awareness of Non-Verbal Cues

If being able to read non-verbal communication cues hasn't always been your strongest forte, then that's okay. It's something that can be learned with a little bit of practice and patience with yourself. It's not going to be easy, and it sure is going to require a whole lot of work, but it's going to be worth it in the end.

Here are some tips on improving your awareness of the non-verbal cues around you:

- **Increase self-awareness**: Pay attention to your own nonverbal cues by observing your facial expressions, body language, and tone of voice. Recognize any patterns or habits that may need adjustment.

- **Observe others**: Practice active observation of nonverbal cues in others. Pay attention to their facial expressions, gestures, and body language to better understand their emotions and intentions.

- **Mirror and match**: When appropriate, subtly mirror the nonverbal cues of the person you are interacting with. This can help establish rapport and create a sense of connection.

- **Practice active listening**: Nonverbal communication is closely tied to active listening. Show genuine interest by maintaining eye contact, nodding, and using appropriate facial expressions to indicate understanding.

- **Seek feedback**: Ask trusted friends, family, or colleagues for feedback on your nonverbal communication. They can provide valuable insights and help you identify areas for improvement.

- **Video self-reflection**: Record yourself in various social situations and review the footage to identify any nonverbal cues that may need adjustment. This can be a helpful tool for self-improvement.

- **Take cues from context**: Consider the cultural and situational context when interpreting and using nonverbal cues. Different cultures may have varying norms and interpretations of nonverbal communication.

- **Practice empathy**: Put yourself in others' shoes and try to understand their perspective. This can help you better interpret their nonverbal cues and respond appropriately.

- **Seek professional help if needed**: There's nothing wrong with reaching out to someone else who knows better. If you struggle significantly with nonverbal communication, consider seeking guidance from a therapist or communication expert who can provide personalized strategies and support.

Addressing Misunderstandings and Miscommunications

Relationships can be a whirlwind of misunderstandings and miscommunications, especially when you have ADHD. It's like a comedy of errors, where even the simplest requests can get lost in translation. I mean, imagine your partner casually mentioning taking out the chicken from the freezer and putting it on the stove. Now, in your ADHD mind, you take it quite literally. You dutifully retrieve the frozen chicken and place it directly on the stove without a pot or any seasoning. It's a hilarious mix-up that perfectly captures the challenges we sometimes face when it comes to communication.

These miscommunications can stem from the unique way in which we process information. Our minds are constantly buzzing with thoughts and ideas, making it easy for details to slip through the cracks. We might hear a request, but our minds may already be on the next thought, causing us to miss important nuances. This can lead to confusion and frustration for both partners.

But it's not just about the ADHD brain. Relationships are a dance of understanding and compromising themselves, and miscommunications happen to everyone. However, for us, these miscommunications can feel more frequent and pronounced. Our tendency to hyperfocus on certain tasks can make us oblivious to the subtleties of communication. We might get so caught up in our own thoughts that we miss the underlying message or intention behind our partner's words.

It's important to remember that these miscommunications are not a reflection of your intelligence or worth. They are simply a part of being human particularly being an ADHD woman navigating relationships. The key is to approach them with humor, patience, and a willingness to learn and grow together.

Typical Miscommunication Scenarios That Can Arise

From seemingly innocent mix-ups to more complex breakdowns, miscommunications can create tension, frustration, and even humor in our relationships. These moments remind us that understanding and effective communication are essential but often elusive. Let's explore a few common examples of miscommunications that can occur in our relationships, shed light on the unique challenges we face, and offer insights on how to bridge the communication gap:

- **The "Yes, but..." Miscommunication**: Your partner asks if you'd like to go out for dinner, and you respond with a hesitant "Yes, but..." Your intention is to suggest an alternative restaurant, but your partner interprets it as disinterest or reluctance to go out at all.

- **The "Assuming Roles" Miscommunication**: You and your partner divide household chores, but due to ADHD-related forgetfulness, you occasionally forget your assigned tasks. Your partner may interpret this as laziness or a lack of commitment when, in reality, it's a result of ADHD challenges.

- **"Reading Between the Lines" Miscommunication**: Your partner makes a casual comment about feeling tired, and you immediately jump into problem-solving mode, suggesting ways to improve their energy levels. However, your partner just wanted empathy and understanding, leaving both of you feeling misunderstood.

- **The "Unspoken Expectations" Miscommunication**: You assume that your partner will remember your upcoming anniversary without explicitly reminding them. When they forget, you feel hurt and disappointed, while your partner is completely unaware of the significance you attached to the date.

- **The Different Communication Styles" Miscommunication**: You prefer direct and straightforward communication, while your partner tends to be more indirect and hints at their needs. This mismatch in communication styles can lead to confusion and frustration, with both of you feeling like you're speaking different languages.

Bridging That Communication Gap

Relationships thrive when we commit to putting communication at the forefront. Sure, each relationship comes with its own unique dynamics and sets of challenges, but sometimes that communication hurdle can seem like the most impossible of mountains to overcome, but it doesn't have to be that way.

One of the first steps in bridging miscommunication gaps is to cultivate self-awareness. For example, if you tend to get easily distracted during conversations, acknowledge this tendency, and make a conscious effort to stay present and focused. By being aware of your strengths and challenges, you can approach conversations with a greater sense of intentionality.

Another crucial aspect of bridging communication gaps is active listening. For instance, if your partner expresses frustration about a long day at work, instead of immediately offering solutions or advice, practice active listening by fully engaging in the conversation. Maintain eye contact, nod to show understanding, and ask open-ended questions to encourage further sharing. By actively listening, you create a space for your partner to feel heard and understood.

Clear and direct communication is key. If you have a specific request or need, be explicit about it. Instead of assuming your partner will pick up on subtle hints, clearly express what you're looking for. This can help prevent misunderstandings and ensure that both partners are on the same page.

It's also important to create an open and non-judgmental space for communication. When your partner shares a concern or expresses vulnerability, respond with empathy and understanding. Avoid criticizing or dismissing their feelings. By creating a safe space, you encourage open and honest communication, making it easier to navigate miscommunications when they arise.

We also need patience and empathy to bridge those miscommunications. I love this African proverb that says, "If you want to go fast, go alone. If you want to go far, go together." This beautifully encapsulates the importance of patience and empathy in navigating miscommunications. It reminds us that building strong and lasting relationships requires us to slow down, listen, and understand each other's perspectives. By embracing patience and empathy, we create a solid foundation for effective communication and deeper connection. It allows us to go beyond quick fixes and short-term solutions and instead embark on a journey of growth and understanding together. For example, if a miscommunication occurs, take a step back and remind yourself that it's not a personal attack. Instead of getting defensive, approach the situation with a sense of humor and a willingness to learn and grow together. By practicing patience and empathy, you can work through miscommunications in a constructive and compassionate manner.

Lastly, seeking professional support can be immensely helpful in bridging communication gaps. Couples therapy gets so stigmatized; what most of us don't understand is that it's not there to shame us or anything like that, but it's meant to help us get closer and build stronger connections with our partners. For example, if miscommunications persist and impact your relationship, consider couples therapy or ADHD coaching. A trained professional can provide guidance, tools, and strategies specifically tailored to your unique relationship dynamics and challenges.

I always tell people that I love them, and I love to see people grow in love. I think that's the most beautiful thing to witness—the shared connection. Divine unity. Where two becomes one. On the journey of love, there will be moments of joy and moments of struggle. But it is in these moments that we have the opportunity to grow, both individually and as a couple. As we continue to explore the intricacies of ADHD in relationships, may we never forget that love is not just about perfection but about embracing imperfections and supporting each other through them?

Chapter 4:

Nurturing Healthy Boundaries

Boundary work is sacred work in our relationships. It is the art of carving out space for our souls to breathe freely, honor our worth, and protect the delicate essence that resides within. In a world that often demands our constant availability and selflessness, nurturing healthy boundaries becomes an act of radical self-love—an act that holds power to transform our lives. Imagine, if you will, a garden left untended, overrun by invasive weeds that suffocate the vibrant blossoms struggling to emerge. Like that forsaken garden, our lives can become tangled in the chaos of others' expectations, desires, and demands. We find ourselves lost in a labyrinth of obligations, burdened by the weight of responsibilities that overshadow our own needs. But within us lies an indomitable spirit, yearning to reclaim its space, shed the suffocating layers, and rediscover its true essence.

Nurturing healthy boundaries is an act of defiance against the societal narratives that tell us we must prioritize everyone else's needs above our own. It is an act of liberation; born from the realization that we are not selfish for seeking a life in harmony with our own desires and dreams. In fact, it is an act of self-preservation, a plea to the universe that we are worthy of respect, understanding, and love.

But boundary work is not without its challenges. As women, we often internalize the notion that setting boundaries is synonymous with being unkind or unloving. We fear the repercussions of asserting our needs and expressing our truths, haunted by the specter of rejection or abandonment. Yet, in denying ourselves the right to establish healthy boundaries, we inadvertently deny our true selves—the radiant souls yearning to be seen and heard.

Picture, for a moment, a sculptor chiseling away at a block of marble. With each deliberate strike of the hammer, she unveils the masterpiece hidden within the raw stone. Similarly, nurturing healthy boundaries is an act of self-sculpting—an act of chiseling away the layers of societal conditioning, fear, and self-doubt that obscure our innate worth. It is a process that requires courage, vulnerability, and unwavering self-belief.

As we embark on this sacred journey of boundary work, we must remember that it is not a solitary endeavor. It is an invitation to communicate openly and honestly with those who inhabit our lives—to share our vulnerabilities, hopes, and boundaries. It is about fostering relationships that honor and uplift us, where our authentic selves are welcomed and celebrated.

In this chapter, we will explore the multifaceted aspects of boundary work—how to recognize our own limits, communicate them effectively, and navigate the inevitable challenges that arise. Together, we will learn to listen, guided by the gentle whispers of self-compassion and the unyielding strength of our inner power.

Types of Boundaries

When we have good boundaries—when our boundaries are healthy—we know just how much time, how much energy, and how much attention to give others. These boundaries are what help us love the people in our lives that much better.

Primarily, boundaries can be categorized into four types: physical, emotional, mental, and time boundaries.

Physical boundaries are perhaps the easiest to understand because they involve our personal space and comfort zones. These are the literal, tangible distances we maintain from others. For instance, you may not want colleagues to enter your personal office without knocking. Or, in a relationship, one partner may not feel comfortable with public displays of affection. By setting and respecting these physical boundaries, we ensure that our personal space is acknowledged and protected.

Emotional boundaries involve managing our feelings and ensuring they are respected by others. They include our right to have and express different emotions. For example, in a friendship, you may feel uncomfortable when a friend constantly dumps their emotional baggage on you without considering your capacity to handle it. Setting an emotional boundary could involve telling them that, while you're there for them, there are times when you need to look after your own emotional well-being first.

Mental boundaries relate to your thoughts, values, opinions, and beliefs. It's about respecting and asserting your right to have and voice your own views, even if they differ from others. Suppose you have a friend who frequently belittles your political beliefs. In this case, a mental boundary could involve expressing to them that you are open to constructive discussions but not to disrespect or mockery.

Time boundaries, while often overlooked, are equally important. They involve designating specific periods for work, leisure, relationships, and self-care. By setting these boundaries, we ensure that we don't overextend ourselves. An example may be setting a rule that you don't answer work emails after 6 p.m. to ensure you have time for rest and personal relationships.

In practice, applying these boundaries in relationships requires open communication and mutual respect. It's about expressing your needs clearly and assertively without infringing on the rights of others.

For instance, if your partner wants to spend every weekend together but you need some time to yourself, a time boundary could be set where you agree to spend one weekend together and the other apart. Similarly, if a friend tends to overshare their problems, causing you emotional distress, you could set an emotional boundary by kindly explaining that there are times when you can't provide the support they need.

Remember, setting boundaries isn't about pushing people away, but rather creating a safe space where everyone's needs and rights are respected. It's a constant negotiation, requiring understanding and patience from all parties involved. By setting and respecting boundaries, we can enrich our relationships, ensuring they provide support, pleasure, and personal growth.

Effectively Communicating Your Boundaries

Imagine standing at the edge of a breathtaking landscape where the vibrant colors of nature blend seamlessly into each other. The air is filled with a sense of tranquility, and the gentle breeze whispers its secrets. In this picturesque scene, we find inspiration on how to express our boundaries in a clear and respectful way.

Just as a skilled painter uses various brushstrokes to create a masterpiece, we too, can employ different techniques to communicate our boundaries effectively. The first step is to understand our own needs and values, as these serve as the foundation for setting boundaries. Like the vibrant colors of the landscape, our boundaries should reflect our authentic selves and what is important to us.

When expressing boundaries, it is crucial to adopt a descriptive approach. Instead of simply stating what we want or don't want, we can paint a vivid picture with words to help others understand our perspective. By using descriptive language, we can articulate our boundaries in a way that resonates with others, just as a beautiful landscape captivates the beholder.

One way to express boundaries clearly is through effective communication. Like a skilled artist who chooses the right hues and shades, we can carefully select our words to convey our boundaries in a respectful manner. By expressing ourselves assertively rather than aggressively, we can avoid causing unnecessary conflict or hurt feelings. Just as the gentle breeze carries its message softly, we can communicate our boundaries in a way that is both firm and kind.

Active listening is another important aspect of expressing boundaries clearly and respectfully. Just as an artist observes every detail of their subject, we should pay close attention to the thoughts and feelings of others. By truly listening, we demonstrate respect and empathy, fostering an environment of open dialogue. This allows us to understand others' perspectives while also ensuring our boundaries are acknowledged and respected.

In addition to effective communication and active listening, it is essential to set boundaries that are realistic and consistent. Just as a well-composed painting follows a consistent theme, our boundaries should be clear and consistent across different situations. This helps others understand our limits and prevents confusion or misunderstandings. By setting boundaries that are grounded in reality, we create a reliable framework for our interactions.

Lastly, expressing boundaries in a clear and respectful way requires self-awareness and self-confidence. Like a skilled painter who trusts their artistic instincts, we must trust ourselves and our judgment. By acknowledging our own worth and valuing our needs, we can confidently communicate our boundaries without fear of rejection or judgment.

Remember, expressing boundaries is an art form in itself. Through effective communication, active listening, consistency, and self-confidence, we can create a masterpiece of respectful and clear boundaries.

Boundary Setting Challenges

Setting boundaries can be a tricky task for anyone, but for individuals with Attention Deficit Hyperactivity Disorder (ADHD), it can present unique challenges. ADHD is a neurodevelopmental disorder characterized by symptoms such as inattention, impulsivity, and hyperactivity. These symptoms can complicate the process of establishing and maintaining boundaries, leading to a range of difficulties in different aspects of life.

One of the primary challenges faced by those of us with ADHD when it comes to setting boundaries is our struggle with impulsivity. People with ADHD often have difficulty inhibiting their immediate reactions and impulses, which can lead to impulsive behaviors or difficulty saying no to others. This impulsivity makes it that much harder for us to assert personal limits and communicate boundaries effectively. We may often find ourselves agreeing to take on additional tasks or responsibilities without considering the impact on our own well-being.

Another challenge stems from the inattentiveness aspect of ADHD. Most of us often have difficulty maintaining focus and attention, which can make it harder for us to recognize when our boundaries are being violated or when we need to establish boundaries in the first place. This can result in a lack of self-awareness regarding personal limits and an increased vulnerability to being taken advantage of or overwhelmed by others' demands.

Most of us with ADHD also struggle with time management and organization. These difficulties can make it challenging to prioritize and allocate time for self-care and boundary-setting activities. They may feel overwhelmed by their daily responsibilities and find it challenging to carve out the necessary time and energy to establish and enforce boundaries effectively.

Moreover, the hyperactivity aspect of ADHD can interfere with boundary-setting efforts. Restlessness and a constant need for movement can make it difficult to maintain the focus needed for clear communication and assertiveness. This can prevent us from effectively expressing our boundaries and needs, leading to misunderstandings and difficulties in our relationships.

Then, there are also the societal misconceptions and stigmas surrounding ADHD that pose challenges. Many people may not fully understand or appreciate the impact that ADHD has on a person's ability to set and maintain boundaries. This lack of understanding can lead to judgment, criticism, or dismissal of their needs, making it even more challenging for individuals with ADHD to assert their boundaries confidently.

Boundaries in Different Relationships

Friends

Personal Space and Time: Imagine yourself engrossed in a captivating novel, yearning for a few moments of solitude. Suddenly, your phone buzzes with an incoming call from a dear friend. While their companionship is valued, it is equally important to assert your need for personal space and time. By respectfully declining their invitation and explaining your desire for solitude, you communicate that you cherish their friendship while honoring your own emotional well-being.

Emotional Availability: Friends often turn to us for support during challenging times, seeking solace within the safety of our bond. However, it is crucial to recognize our own emotional limits and set boundaries accordingly. For instance, if a friend consistently leans on you for emotional support without reciprocation, you may need to communicate your need for a more balanced dynamic. By expressing your feelings honestly and lovingly, you foster an environment of mutual understanding and growth.

Family

Respectful Communication: Family ties are deep-rooted and often intertwined with complex emotions and histories. When engaging in conversations with family members, it is vital to set boundaries around respectful communication. For instance, if a family member consistently belittles your achievements or crosses personal boundaries, you can firmly but kindly express your discomfort. By doing so, you assert your worth and establish a foundation for healthier interactions.

Time Commitments: Family gatherings and obligations can consume significant portions of our time and energy. While familial bonds are precious, it is crucial to strike a balance between meeting familial responsibilities and preserving personal well-being. By respectfully declining certain commitments or negotiating alternative arrangements, you ensure that your own needs are met, cultivating both self-care and family harmony.

Boundaries With Colleagues

Work-Life Balance: In today's fast-paced work environments, maintaining a healthy work-life balance is paramount. Setting boundaries with colleagues can be crucial to safeguarding your personal life. For example, you might establish clear expectations around after-work availability, ensuring that your personal time remains protected. Communicating these boundaries assertively yet respectfully allows you to recharge and bring your best self to both your personal and professional spheres.

Task Distribution: Collaboration is a cornerstone of many workplaces, but it can lead to an uneven distribution of tasks, creating stress and imbalance. By setting boundaries around task distribution and workload, you assert your value and contribute to a more equitable work environment. Communicating your preferences, strengths, and limitations allows for a fairer allocation of responsibilities, fostering greater productivity and job satisfaction.

When Our Boundaries Get Crossed

When we set our boundaries, it is with the hope that the people we hold dear will respect and honor them. Boundaries serve as the framework within which we define our needs, desires, and limits. They act as a safeguard, protecting our emotional, mental, and physical well-being. But what happens when those we love—our friends, family, or colleagues—cross those boundaries?

It can be a disheartening experience, one that challenges our sense of self and the trust we have placed in our relationships. We may find ourselves grappling with feelings of confusion, frustration, and even resentment. It is during these times that we must navigate a delicate balance between asserting ourselves and preserving the connection we have with these individuals.

In situations like these, it is important to first reflect on our own boundaries and ensure that they are communicated clearly and effectively. Sometimes, those around us may not even be aware of the lines we have drawn. Taking the initiative to express our needs and expectations can pave the way for healthier, more respectful interactions.

When faced with the crossing of boundaries, we should resist the urge to react impulsively or withdraw from the relationship altogether. Instead, we should seek to understand the motives behind their actions. Often, these breaches are not intentional or malicious but rather a result of differing perspectives, unawareness, or personal struggles.

Approaching the conversation with empathy and compassion can foster a safe environment for open dialogue. Through effective communication, we can express how their actions have impacted us and work towards finding a compromise that respects both parties involved.

We have to remember that boundary crossing does not define the entirety of a relationship. Our loved ones, although imperfect, possess qualities and virtues that make them valuable to us. Recognizing the complexities of human interactions allows us to have realistic expectations and better navigate these challenging situations.

When Boundary-Setting Gets Hard: Things to Remember

- **Remember that setting boundaries is an act of self-care**: Remind yourself that boundaries are not selfish but rather a necessary element of maintaining your well-being and happiness.

- **Embrace the discomfort**: Recognize that setting boundaries often involves stepping outside of your comfort zone. Embrace the challenge as an opportunity for personal growth and increased self-awareness.

- **Be clear and assertive in your communication**: Clearly express your boundaries in a confident and respectful manner. Avoid being passive or assuming others will understand your needs without direct communication.

- **Understand that boundary crossing is not a reflection of your worth**: When others disregard your boundaries, it is important to remember that their actions do not define your value or worthiness. Their behavior is a reflection of their own struggles and limitations.

- **Seek support**: Reach out to trusted friends, family, or therapists who can provide guidance and encouragement. Surrounding yourself with a supportive network can make navigating difficult boundary-setting situations easier.

- **Practice self-compassion**: Be kind to yourself throughout this process. Acknowledge that boundary setting can be challenging and that it's okay to make mistakes. Treat yourself with the same understanding and compassion you offer to others.

- **Establish consequences for boundary violations**: what are you planning on doing when your people do not respect your boundaries as they should? Clearly communicate the consequences of crossing your boundaries. This can help reinforce the importance of respecting your limits and may encourage others to reconsider their actions.

- **Set realistic expectations**: We have to remember that when we are setting boundaries, we are dealing with human beings. Understand that not everyone will meet your boundaries consistently. People have different perspectives and struggles. Instead of expecting perfection, focus on progress and open communication.

- **Celebrate small victories**: When I set a boundary and win at it, I do something small for myself to remind me of what an incredible thing that is. Recognize and celebrate the moments when others respect and honor your boundaries. These triumphs serve as reminders of your own growth and the positive impact of boundary setting.

Remember that boundary setting is an ongoing process. Boundaries may need to be reassessed and adjusted over time as circumstances and relationships evolve. Embrace the journey of self-discovery and adapt your boundaries accordingly.

Chapter 5:

Managing Time and Priorities

So, right now, you're on a mission to find your misplaced keys, but as you search frantically, you notice your phone buzzing with notifications. Without skipping a beat, you answer a call while continuing your quest for the elusive keys. Suddenly, you find yourself in a comical dance, twirling around the room with your phone in one hand and a magnifying glass in the other, desperately trying to locate both your keys and your sanity.

Meanwhile, your to-do list stares back at you, mocking your attempts at time management. It's as if the universe has conspired to turn your life into a never-ending game of hide-and-seek. But hey, at least you've become a master of multitasking, even when it doesn't make logical sense.

In the midst of this chaos, you realize that your ADHD brain is wired for adventure and spontaneity. While others may see your struggles with time management as a hindrance, you embrace it as a unique superpower. Who needs a boring, predictable schedule when you can navigate through life like a fearless explorer, always ready for the next unexpected twist?

Sure, there may be moments of frustration and the occasional mix-up of priorities, but you've learned to laugh at the absurdity of it all. After all, life is too short to take everything so seriously. So, as you continue your quest for time management mastery, remember to embrace the quirks and unpredictability that come with being an ADHD woman. Who knows, maybe one day you'll find your keys and conquer that to-do list, all while keeping a smile on your face and a twinkle in your eye.

Time Management Challenges in Relationships

Time management challenges will really sneak up on us, like that friend who always shows up unannounced and overstays their welcome. We may not even realize it, but these sneaky challenges can wreak havoc on our relationships with our partners. From increased stress and frustration to emotional impacts on intimacy and connection, let's dive into some examples of how time management challenges can affect our love lives.

Increased Stress and Frustration

Imagine this scenario: You and your partner plan a romantic dinner date to celebrate a special occasion. However, due to poor time management, you find yourself rushing through preparations, running late, and feeling stressed. As a result, the atmosphere becomes tense, and the initial excitement and joy of the occasion are overshadowed by frustration. Instead of enjoying each other's company, you find yourselves bickering over trivial things. A lack of time management not only steals away your peace but also chips away at the harmony of your relationship.

Emotional Impact on Intimacy and Connection

Let's say you and your partner have been longing for some quality time together. However, your busy schedules and poor time management skills constantly get in the way. You both feel emotionally disconnected and find it challenging to nurture your intimacy. The lack of shared moments and meaningful conversations can create a void in your relationship, leading to feelings of loneliness and dissatisfaction. Without proper time management, the flame of passion may dwindle, and the emotional bond between you and your partner may weaken.

Strained Trust

Trust is the foundation of any healthy relationship. Now, picture this: You promise your partner that you'll be home early to spend the evening together. However, due to poor time management and a series of unforeseen circumstances, you arrive hours later than expected. Your partner's trust in your commitment and reliability may take a hit.

Doubts may creep in, and they might wonder if they can count on you in the future. Time management challenges can strain trust by undermining the belief that you value and prioritize your partner's time and needs.

Navigating time management challenges in relationships requires open communication, understanding, and a willingness to make adjustments. By acknowledging the impact these challenges can have, we can take proactive steps to address them.

Struggling With Prioritization

Prioritization is the eternal struggle that many women with ADHD face. It's like trying to wrangle a herd of cats while juggling flaming torches—a true balancing act that can have some not-so-pleasant consequences. But why do we struggle so much with prioritizing and creating proper balance in our schedules?

Well, simply put, life's a circus. For many of us, life can sometimes feel like being the ringmaster of a never-ending circus. Between work, family, friends, hobbies, and a million other things vying for attention, it's no wonder our prioritization skills get a bit wobbly. We may find ourselves getting easily distracted, jumping from one task to another like an over-caffeinated squirrel, and struggling to focus on what truly matters. It's like trying to tame a lion while a bunch of clowns juggle in the background—pure chaos!

Now, let's shine the spotlight on how this impacts our relationships. Picture this: You're supposed to meet your partner for a romantic dinner, but your ADHD brain has other plans. Suddenly, you're knee-deep in a project you forgot about, lost track of time, and left your partner hanging. They may feel neglected, frustrated, or even hurt by your unintentional forgetfulness. It's like having a trapeze act without a safety net—things can quickly go south from there!

But I'm not going to leave you hanging without any suggestions. Here are five tips for taming the ADHD circus:

1. **Embrace the power of lists**: Creating to-do lists or using digital task management apps can be lifesavers. Write down your tasks, prioritize them, and tackle them one by one. It's like having a trusty assistant with an elephant-like memory.

2. **Break it down**: Large tasks can feel overwhelming, so break them down into smaller, more manageable steps. It's like dividing a daring high-wire act into a series of smaller jumps— less daunting, more achievable.

3. **Set reminders and alarms**: Use technology to your advantage! Set reminders and alarms on your phone or other devices to help you stay on track. It's like having a personal circus announcer shout, "Don't forget! Time to focus on this task!"

4. **Delegate and ask for help**: You don't have to be a one-woman show. Don't hesitate to delegate tasks or ask for help when needed. Remember, even the greatest circus acts have a talented support team behind the scenes.

5. **Practice self-compassion**: Cut yourself some slack, my fellow ADHD circus performers. Remember that you're doing your best. If you stumble or drop a few balls, it's okay. Laugh it off, pick them up, and keep going. After all, the show must go on!

Procrastination

Ah, procrastination—the art of putting things off until the last possible moment. It's a struggle that many of us face, and for those with ADHD, it can sometimes feel like we've earned a Ph.D. in the subject.

Procrastination often goes hand in hand with ADHD due to a combination of factors. Our brains crave novelty and stimulation, so tasks that are repetitive or mundane can easily lose interest. We may also struggle with executive functioning skills such as organizing, prioritizing, and maintaining focus. As a result, we find ourselves dancing with procrastination, postponing important tasks in favor of immediate gratification or more engaging activities.

Empowering Strategies to Combat Procrastination

- **Break It Down**: One of the biggest obstacles to starting a task is feeling overwhelmed by its magnitude. Break it down into smaller, manageable steps. By focusing on one step at a time, you'll reduce the overwhelming feeling and create momentum.

- **Set Clear Goals and Deadlines**: Define specific goals and assign realistic deadlines for yourself. Having a clear target and a sense of urgency can provide the necessary motivation to get started and stay on track.

- **Use Visual Reminders**: Keep visual cues or reminders of your tasks in prominent places. Sticky notes, calendars, or digital reminders can serve as gentle nudges to keep you accountable and focused on what needs to be done.

- **Harness the Power of Rewards**: Create a reward system for yourself. After completing a task or reaching a milestone, treat yourself to something you enjoy. It could be a short break, a small indulgence, or engaging in a favorite activity. Rewards can help incentivize progress and make the process more enjoyable.

- **Find Your Optimal Environment**: Identify the environment where you feel most focused and productive. It could be a quiet corner of your home, a local café, or a library. Experiment and discover what works best for you to minimize distractions and maximize productivity.

- **Utilize Accountability Partners**: Share your goals and progress with someone you trust. An accountability partner can provide support, encouragement, and gentle reminders to keep you on track. They can serve as your personal cheerleader in the fight against procrastination.

- **Practice Self-Compassion**: Remember, we're all humans and occasional bouts of procrastination are natural. Instead of beating yourself up over it, practice self-compassion.

Acknowledge that it happens, let go of any guilt or self-judgment, focus on the present moment, and take action.

Creating Balance in Personal and Professional Relationships

Balance is something we all talk about, but it's quite difficult to create. I used to be one of those people, constantly struggling to find equilibrium in my personal and professional relationships. As a woman with ADHD, the challenges were magnified, and I often found myself feeling overwhelmed and stretched thin.

One particular incident stands out in my memory, a moment that served as a wake-up call and propelled me on a journey towards finding balance. It was a sunny afternoon, and I had just returned home from a long and exhausting day at work. As I stepped through the front door, I was greeted by the sight of my partner, Sarah, sitting on the couch, her face etched with disappointment.

I knew something was wrong, but my mind was still buzzing with the demands of the day. I tried to focus on her words, but my attention kept drifting, pulled in a thousand different directions. It was as if my brain was a tangled web of thoughts, preventing me from fully engaging in the conversation.

Sarah's frustration grew, and tears welled up in her eyes. She expressed how she felt neglected and unimportant as if my work had taken precedence over our relationship. In that moment, I felt a deep pang of guilt and regret. How had I let myself become so consumed by my professional life that I had neglected the person I loved?

It was a turning point for me. I realized that I needed to make a change and find a way to create balance between my personal and professional life. I began by seeking support and guidance, reaching out to therapists, coaches, and fellow ADHD women who had faced similar struggles.

Through self-reflection and a commitment to personal growth, I started implementing strategies to manage my time and energy more effectively. I learned to set boundaries, both at work and in my personal life, allowing myself dedicated moments of rest and connection. I discovered the power of mindfulness and meditation, practices that helped me quiet the chaos in my mind and be fully present in my relationships.

Slowly but surely, I began to see the positive impact of these changes. Sarah noticed the difference, too, as our connection deepened, and our bond grew stronger. I no longer felt like a ship lost at sea, constantly battling the waves of distraction and overwhelm. Instead, I found a sense of harmony, a delicate dance between my personal and professional lives.

This journey towards balance is ongoing, and I still face challenges along the way. But I am grateful for that pivotal moment, that wake-up call that pushed me to prioritize my relationships and find the equilibrium I had been yearning for. It is my hope that by sharing my story, others like you can find inspiration and guidance on their own path towards creating balance in their lives.

Tips on Creating Balance in Relationships

- **Prioritize self-care**: Take care of yourself by engaging in activities that recharge you, such as exercise, hobbies, or relaxation. For example, you can dedicate an hour each morning to meditation and journaling, starting the day with a clear mind and a sense of calm.

- **Set boundaries**: Establish clear boundaries to prevent work from encroaching on personal time. Communicate your availability and limits to colleagues and loved ones. For instance, you can turn off work notifications during family dinners, ensuring uninterrupted quality time with your partner and children.

- **Practice effective time management**: Efficiently manage your time by prioritizing tasks, delegating when possible, and avoiding overcommitment. For example, you can use a time-blocking technique to allocate specific time slots for work, family, and personal activities, staying organized and preventing overwhelm.

- **Foster open communication**: Cultivate healthy relationships through open and honest communication. Regularly check in with your loved ones and colleagues to ensure everyone's needs are being met. For instance, you can implement a weekly "relationship check-in" where you discuss any concerns or issues, addressing potential imbalances and finding solutions together.

- **Practice active listening**: Fully engage in conversations by giving your full attention and avoiding distractions. For example, put away your phone and maintain eye contact when your friends or family members are sharing their thoughts or feelings, actively listening, and deepening your relationships.

- **Learn to delegate and ask for help**: Recognize that you don't have to do everything alone. Delegate tasks at work and ask for support from loved ones when needed. For instance, you can ask your partner to take on more household responsibilities, allowing you to spend more quality time with your children and reducing overall stress.

- **Practice mindfulness**: Stay present in the moment to fully engage in personal and professional interactions. Incorporate mindfulness techniques, such as deep breathing or grounding exercises, to stay calm and attentive. For example, you can take short mindfulness breaks throughout your workday, helping you stay centered and improving your relationships with colleagues.

- **Practice empathy and understanding**: Put yourself in the shoes of others to foster compassion and strengthen your relationships. For instance, when you notice a colleague seems overwhelmed, take the time to listen and offer support, creating a more supportive and balanced work environment.

- **Schedule quality time**: Make intentional plans to spend quality time with loved ones. For example, you can establish a weekly date night with your partner or plan family outings on the weekends, prioritizing these moments for connection and strengthening your personal relationships.

- **Learn to say "no:"** Recognize your limits and practice saying no to commitments that don't align with your priorities or values. For example, when asked to take on an additional project at work, politely decline, knowing that it would compromise your personal time and relationships.

- **Create boundaries around technology**: Set boundaries around your use of devices to prevent technology from interfering with your personal relationships. For instance, implement a rule of no phones at the dinner table, ensuring uninterrupted quality time with your loved ones.

Communicating and Negotiating Priorities With Partners

Negotiating with our partners is not always easy, but it is crucial, especially for individuals with ADHD. Let me introduce you to Sarah and Alex, a couple navigating the challenges of ADHD together.

Sarah and Alex had been together for several years, and while they loved each other deeply, they often found themselves at odds when it came to household responsibilities. Sarah, who had ADHD, struggled with maintaining a consistent cleaning routine, while Alex, who was more organized, felt overwhelmed by the constant clutter.

One evening, after a particularly frustrating day, they decided it was time to have an open and honest conversation about their differing expectations. They sat down at the kitchen table, ready to negotiate and find a compromise that would work for both of them.

Sarah began by expressing her challenges with organization and how they affected her ability to keep the house tidy. She shared her frustrations and acknowledged the impact it had on their relationship. Alex listened attentively, understanding the difficulties Sarah faced due to her ADHD.

In turn, Alex expressed their need for a clean and organized living space, explaining how it contributed to their overall well-being and reduced their own stress levels. They emphasized that it wasn't about perfection but rather a shared responsibility for maintaining a comfortable home environment.

With a newfound understanding of each other's perspectives, Sarah and Alex began exploring potential solutions. They brainstormed ideas that would address both their needs and create a compromise that felt fair and manageable.

They decided to divide the household tasks based on their strengths and preferences. Sarah took on responsibilities that aligned more with her strengths, such as cooking and grocery shopping, while Alex focused on organizing and tidying up the shared spaces. They agreed to set aside specific times each week for joint cleaning sessions, where they would tackle larger tasks together.

To support Sarah's ADHD challenges, they implemented visual reminders, such as a chore chart and shared calendar, to help her stay on track with her tasks. They also established regular check-ins to assess how their system was working and make adjustments as needed.

Through negotiation and compromise, Sarah and Alex found a solution that worked for both of them. They recognized that it wasn't about one person being right or wrong, but rather finding a middle ground that respected their individual strengths and accommodated their unique challenges.

As a result, their relationship flourished. The shared responsibilities and understanding fostered a sense of teamwork and support. Sarah felt less overwhelmed by the household tasks, and Alex appreciated the effort Sarah put into managing her ADHD symptoms.

Negotiating and finding compromises became a regular practice for Sarah and Alex. It allowed them to navigate their ADHD challenges together, strengthening their bond and creating a more harmonious and balanced partnership.

How to Stop Overcommitting Yourself

Have you ever found yourself in a situation where you realized that you said "yes" to one too many things, and now you're juggling more commitments than a circus performer? It happens to the best of us! While overcommitting ourselves might seem like a recurring theme in our lives, let's explore some reasons why we tend to take on more than we can handle.

The Superhero Syndrome: We all secretly believe we possess superhuman powers capable of accomplishing anything. When someone asks for our help or invites us to an event, our inner superhero jumps to the rescue, thinking, "I can totally handle this!" We say "yes" without considering the time or energy required, only to realize later that we're not quite as invincible as we thought.

The Fear of Missing Out (FOMO): Ah, FOMO, the sneaky culprit that convinces us we'll miss out on life's greatest adventures if we decline an invitation. We imagine the incredible stories we'll hear and the amazing experiences we'll have, so we eagerly agree to everything. But then reality hits, and we realize that attending multiple events simultaneously is not yet scientifically possible.

The People-Pleaser Predicament: We're social creatures who crave approval and validation from others. Saying "no" can sometimes feel like letting people down, disappointing them, or worse, making them think we're not helpful or reliable. So, we agree to everything to maintain our reputation as the ultimate dependable friend, partner, or colleague. Little do we know that spreading ourselves too thin can actually lead to the opposite effect.

The Illusion of Time Multiplication: Time seems to play tricks on us. We fall into the illusion that we have more than 24 hours in a day, believing we can squeeze in an extra commitment here and there without any consequences. We convince ourselves that we can magically expand time or somehow manipulate the space-time continuum. Unfortunately, reality strikes, and we're faced with the harsh truth that time is, indeed, finite.

While it's great to be enthusiastic and helpful, it's essential to balance our commitments and learn to say "no" when necessary. After all, we're only humans, and even superheroes need their well-deserved rest! Here are some tips that you can start implementing to help you create that fine line between too much and just enough:

- **Pause and reflect**: Before immediately saying "yes" to a new commitment, take a moment to pause and reflect. Assess your current workload, obligations, and personal priorities. Consider whether you have the time, energy, and resources to take on something new without sacrificing your well-being or neglecting existing commitments.

- **Practice the art of prioritization**: Learn to prioritize your commitments based on their importance and alignment with your goals. Focus on tasks and activities that truly matter to you and have a significant impact on your life. By identifying your priorities, you can make more informed decisions about what to say "yes" to and what to decline.

- **Embrace the power of "no:"** Saying "no" is not a bad thing. It's an essential skill that allows you to set boundaries and protect your time and energy. Practice saying "no" politely and assertively when a new commitment doesn't align with your priorities or when you simply don't have the capacity to take it on. Remember, saying "no" to one thing means saying "yes" to something else that matters more.

- **Delegate and collaborate**: Recognize that you don't have to do everything on your own. Learn to delegate tasks or seek collaboration when appropriate. Sharing responsibilities not only lighten your load but also allows others to contribute their skills and expertise. Whether it's at work or in your personal life, don't hesitate to ask for help and share the workload.

- **Set realistic expectations:** Be honest with yourself and others about what you can realistically accomplish within a given timeframe. Avoid overestimating your capacity or underestimating the time required for tasks. By setting realistic expectations, you'll reduce the likelihood of overcommitting and feeling overwhelmed.

- **Learn to negotiate**: If you're interested in a commitment but feel unsure about your capacity to take it on fully, explore the option of negotiation. Discuss with the person or group making the request and find a compromise that works for both parties. This could involve adjusting deadlines, reducing the scope of the commitment, or collaborating with others to share the workload.

Accountability as a Time Management Tool

Accountability is your trusty sidekick, always there to support you on your time management adventures. As a woman with ADHD, juggling multiple responsibilities can sometimes feel like trying to herd cats. That's where accountability swoops in, ready to lend a helping hand.

Imagine it like this: Accountability is your secret weapon—a friendly guide who keeps you on track and ensures you stay focused on your goals. It's like having a personal cheerleader and a gentle nudge all rolled into one. When you embrace it, you invite someone or something into your life that holds you responsible for your actions, progress, and commitments.

For us, women with ADHD, accountability is particularly valuable. It provides structure, consistency, and external support to counteract the challenges that come with ADHD. Here's why it matters:

- **Anchoring your focus**: ADHD often brings a whirlwind of distractions and difficulty maintaining focus. Accountability acts as an anchor, helping you stay centered and directing your attention to what truly matters. When you know someone is counting on you or tracking your progress, it becomes easier to resist distractions and stay on task.

- **Aiding in consistency**: Consistency can be a struggle when ADHD makes it challenging to establish routines and stick to them. Accountability provides the gentle reminders and encouragement needed to develop consistent habits. By being accountable to someone or something, you create external structure and support that nudges you towards maintaining regularity in your actions.

- **Overcoming procrastination**: Procrastination can be a persistent companion. Accountability is like your personal anti-procrastination coach. When you have someone checking in on your progress, it becomes harder to delay tasks or succumb to the allure of distractions. Accountability keeps you motivated, nudging you to take action and break through the cycle of procrastination.

- **Celebrating achievements**: ADHD can sometimes overshadow your accomplishments, making it easy to overlook your successes. Accountability helps shine a light on your achievements, big or small. By sharing your progress with someone who supports and acknowledges your efforts, you gain a sense of accomplishment and motivation to keep going. Celebrating wins boosts your confidence and reinforces positive behaviors.

Ultimately, accountability is about recognizing that you don't have to navigate the challenges of ADHD alone. It's about finding a system or a person who understands your unique struggles and can provide the support and structure you need. Whether it's a trusted friend, a support group, a coach, or a combination of strategies, embracing accountability can be a game-changer for women with ADHD, helping you unlock your potential and thrive in managing your time effectively.

Techniques for Organizing Schedules, Tasks, and Responsibilities

Organization and schedules are not traits that come naturally to those of us with ADHD. The constant whirlwind of thoughts and the challenges of managing time and tasks can often feel overwhelming, making it difficult to maintain a sense of structure and order.

For an ADHD woman, daily life can be a constant struggle to stay on top of responsibilities, appointments, and commitments. Time slips away like sand through our fingers, and despite our best efforts, she finds herself frequently running late or forgetting important tasks. It's not that we don't care about being negligent; our brains simply process information and manage time differently.

The need for external support and strategies to combat these challenges becomes essential. Whether it's utilizing reminders on a smartphone, setting up visual calendars, or seeking help from understanding friends and family, finding effective systems for organization and schedules can make a significant difference in our lives. Let's have a look at some of those.

Techniques for Keeping Your Schedule Organized

- **Utilize a Digital Calendar**: One effective technique is to use a digital calendar on your smartphone or computer. Apps like Google Calendar or Microsoft Outlook allow you to schedule appointments, set reminders, and sync your calendar across devices. By using a digital calendar, you can easily access and update your schedule, ensuring that you never miss an important event or task. For example, let's say you have a doctor's appointment next week. You can schedule it in your digital calendar, set a reminder a day or two in advance, and even add notes or attach relevant documents to the event. This way, you have all the necessary information in one place and can stay organized.

- **Break Tasks Into Smaller Steps**: Dividing larger tasks into smaller, manageable steps is another helpful technique. It's easy to feel overwhelmed when faced with a complex project or a lengthy to-do list. By breaking tasks down, you can focus on one step at a time, making the process less daunting. Imagine you have a research paper to write. Instead of thinking about it as one big task, break it into smaller steps such as researching, outlining, drafting, editing, and proofreading. This approach not only helps with time management but also provides a sense of accomplishment as you complete each step.

- **Prioritize and Set Realistic Goals**: Prioritization is key to managing your schedule effectively. Identify the most important tasks or deadlines and tackle those first. This ensures that you focus on what truly matters and avoid getting sidetracked by less significant or less time-sensitive obligations. Setting realistic goals is also crucial. Be honest with yourself about what you can realistically achieve in a given day or week. Instead of overloading your schedule, prioritize the most essential tasks and allocate sufficient time for each. By setting achievable goals, you're more likely to stay on track and maintain a sense of organization.

- **Use Color Coding or Labeling Systems**: Visual cues can be helpful for organization. Consider color-coding your tasks or using labeling systems to categorize different types of activities. For example, you could assign specific colors to different projects, personal commitments, or household chores. By visually separating and distinguishing tasks, you can quickly identify priorities and see how your time is allocated. This technique works well for visual learners who benefit from clear visual cues and like to have a visual overview of their schedule.

- **Allocate Buffer Time**: Sometimes unexpected events or delays can disrupt your schedule. To accommodate these unforeseen circumstances, it's essential to allocate buffer time between tasks or appointments. This allows flexibility and prevents a minor interruption from derailing your entire day. For instance, if you have back-to-back meetings, leaving no time in between, any delay in one meeting would cause a domino effect for the subsequent ones. By allocating buffer time, you give yourself breathing room and the ability to handle unforeseen situations without feeling overwhelmed.

- **Regularly Review and Adjust**: Lastly, regularly reviewing and adjusting your schedule is crucial. Take a few minutes at the end of each day or week to evaluate your progress, reassess priorities, and make any necessary adjustments for the upcoming period. For example, if you notice that certain tasks always take longer than anticipated, adjust your schedule accordingly by allocating more time to those activities. Regularly reviewing and adjusting your schedule helps you stay adaptable, manage your time effectively, and ensure that you're meeting your goals.

Remember, finding the techniques that work best for you may require some trial and error. Experiment with different approaches and be patient with yourself as you develop a routine that suits your needs and helps you stay organized.

That's it; we're at the end of another chapter. I'm really excited about this next chapter; it's all about intimacy. Go grab a cup of coffee, and when you're back, let's tackle it together.

Chapter 6:

Enhancing Intimacy and Emotional Connection

Emotional intimacy is a profound, invisible thread that weaves through our relationships, binding us to others with an enchanting strength that often surpasses the physical. It's the feeling of being truly seen, understood, and accepted by another person, of being loved not in spite of our flaws and quirks but because of them. The ability to share our deepest fears, dreams, and desires without fear of judgment or rejection is the essence of emotional intimacy.

It's the quiet understanding, the shared laughter, and the comfort in silence. It's the reassuring squeeze of a hand, the warm hug on a cold night, and the knowing looks exchanged across a crowded room. Emotional intimacy fosters trust and security, providing a safe space for vulnerability where we can shed our armor and be our authentic selves.

In the context of ADHD, emotional intimacy can be both challenging and rewarding. Women with ADHD often process emotions differently, experiencing them more intensely, which can lead to strong bonds and deep connections but also to misunderstandings and conflicts.

Emotional intimacy matters because it nurtures our inherent need for connection. We are social beings, and we thrive on connections that go beyond the surface. When we experience emotional intimacy, we feel seen, heard, and valued. This sense of belonging not only enhances our relationships but also bolsters our self-esteem and overall mental health.

Moreover, emotional intimacy is essential for the longevity and satisfaction of relationships. It is the foundation upon which we build partnerships that can weather life's storms. It's the glue that holds us together when the initial spark fades, and the depth of feeling can turn a fleeting romance into a lifetime love story.

For women with ADHD, cultivating emotional intimacy can be a journey of self-discovery. It means learning to navigate their unique emotional landscape and communicate their needs effectively. It's about being open about their ADHD and how it affects them and finding a partner who is willing to understand and support them.

In the dance of emotional intimacy, we learn to balance our needs with those of others, to listen as much as we speak, and to understand as much as we want to be understood. It's a delicate balance that requires patience, understanding, and, most of all, love.

In the end, emotional intimacy is more than just a component of our relationships. It's a beautiful testament to our capacity for love and understanding, a beacon of hope that reminds us that in a world often marked by disconnection, we can find unity in our shared humanity. It's not just about finding someone who can live with us, but someone who can understand our chaos, share in our passions, and journey with us on this unpredictable ride called life. Intimacy, in its purest form, is a celebration of our shared vulnerability—the realization that in our flaws, we find our most authentic connections.

The Impact of ADHD on Relationship Intimacy

The symptoms of ADHD, such as impulsivity, inattentiveness, and emotional dysregulation, can have a profound impact on the intimacy shared between partners. In this section, we look into the intricate ways ADHD can influence the depth, connection, and overall experience of intimacy within relationships.

- **Dance of presence**: Intimacy thrives on deep emotional connection and being fully present with your partner. However, we often find it difficult to be fully present in the moment. Our minds may wander, and distractions can hijack our attention, leading to a sense of detachment during intimate moments. For example, during a romantic dinner, an individual with ADHD might struggle to maintain sustained focus on their partner, inadvertently conveying a lack of interest or engagement. This can leave our partners feeling unimportant and emotionally disconnected.

- **Impulsivity and sexual expression**: ADHD's impulsive nature can extend into the realm of sexual intimacy, impacting the shared experiences within a relationship. The struggle with self-control is no secret, often leading to impulsive behaviors that can disrupt the natural flow of intimacy. For instance, you might initiate sexual activity without considering your partner's readiness or boundaries, potentially creating discomfort or resentment. This impulsivity can blur the boundaries of consent and compromise the trust necessary for a healthy sexual relationship.

- **Emotional regulation and vulnerability**: Intimacy requires vulnerability and emotional openness. However, ADHD often makes us grapple with emotional regulation, experiencing intense mood swings or difficulty expressing our emotions effectively. This can hinder our ability to connect deeply with our partner on an emotional level. For example, during a heartfelt conversation about your feelings, you may struggle to articulate your emotions, leaving your partner feeling frustrated or disconnected. The fluctuating emotional landscape can create an atmosphere of unpredictability, making it challenging for partners to feel secure in the relationship.

- **Hyperfocus and neglected intimacy**: ADHD's characteristic hyperfocus, while often a double-edged sword, can also have a significant impact on intimacy. When we become fixated on a particular interest or project, we may unintentionally neglect our partner's emotional and physical needs. This can result in a lack of quality time, diminished affection, or a sense of emotional distance. For instance, you might become consumed by a work project, devoting long hours to it and inadvertently neglecting your partner's longing for connection and intimacy.

Techniques and Tips for Opening an Emotional Connection

Love languages, a term that has its origins in Dr. Gary Chapman's book *The Five Love Languages: How to Express Heartfelt Commitment to Your Mate*, are essentially the ways in which we express and interpret love. They are the dialects of the heart, the different channels through which our emotions flow and become tangible to the ones we love. Understanding your partner's love language is akin to unlocking a secret door into their heart to comprehend what truly makes them feel loved, cherished, and understood.

The five love languages, as described by Dr. Chapman, are:

1. Words of Affirmation

This love language uses words to affirm, appreciate, and express love. For those who communicate love in this way, a heartfelt "I love you," a compliment, a word of encouragement, or a written note of affection means more than any gift. It's as if each syllable is a brush stroke, painting a vibrant picture of love and adoration that resonates deep within them.

Things that you can do for a partner who wants to be loved in this way:

- Compliment them regularly and sincerely.

- Write them love notes or letters expressing your feelings.

- Send them thoughtful and uplifting text messages throughout the day.

- Verbally express your appreciation for their efforts and qualities.

- Leave them voice messages or record sweet messages for them to listen to.

- Publicly acknowledge and praise their achievements or acts of kindness.

- Use positive and encouraging words during conversations.

- Remind them of your love and affection frequently.

- Leave sticky notes with loving messages in places they'll find them.

- Speak kind and affirming words about them to others.

2. Acts of Service

Doing something for your partner that you know they would like, such as cooking a meal, washing dishes, or picking up a prescription, are all acts of service. They require thought, time, and effort. For those whose primary love language is acts of service, these actions are like a symphony of love; each act is a note that forms a beautiful melody of affection and dedication. How can you love your partner well in this way?

- Take care of tasks or chores they usually handle to lighten their load.

- Prepare their favorite meal or surprise them with breakfast in bed.

- Offer to run errands or handle responsibilities on their behalf.

- Plan a special date or outing that caters to their preferences and interests.

- Help them with a project or task they've been wanting to complete.

- Offer to give them a massage or pamper them in some way.

- Take care of their responsibilities or obligations to give them some time for relaxation.

- Offer to do something they dislike doing, such as cleaning or organizing.

- Support their goals or dreams by assisting them in any way you can.

- Show up and be present when they need your help or support.

3. Receiving Gifts

For some, what makes them feel most loved is to receive a gift. The cost of the gift is irrelevant, but the thoughtfulness behind it is what counts. A perfectly chosen gift is like a treasure, a tangible token of love that they can hold, something that captures the essence of their partner's affection in a form that they can touch and see.

- Thoughtfully select and give them meaningful gifts that align with their interests and preferences.

- Surprise them with small tokens of affection or appreciation.

- Pay attention to items they mention wanting or needing and surprise them with those.

- Plan special occasions or celebrations where they can receive gifts.

- Create personalized gifts or handmade items that hold sentimental value.

- Give them experiences or outings that they would enjoy.

- Show excitement and gratitude when receiving gifts from them.

- Remember important dates and occasions and celebrate them with thoughtful gifts.

- Consider their love for surprises and occasionally surprise them with unexpected gifts.

- Be attentive to their reactions and expressions when receiving gifts, as it can provide insight into their preferences and desires.

4. Quality Time

This language is all about undivided attention. No televisions, no smartphones, or any other distractions. If this is your partner's primary language, they don't just want to be around you; they want to be true to you, sharing experiences and time. It's as if each shared moment is a precious gem, a sparkling testament to the bond you share.

- Prioritize spending uninterrupted and focused time together.

- Engage in activities that they enjoy and actively participate in them.

- Plan regular date nights or outings to create special moments.

- Have meaningful conversations and actively listen to them.

- Put away distractions like phones or electronics during your quality time.

- Show genuine interest in their hobbies, interests, and experiences.

- Take turns planning surprises or activities for each other.

- Create rituals or traditions that you can enjoy together.

- Plan vacations or getaways to spend extended quality time together.

- Be fully present and make an effort to connect emotionally during your time together.

5. Physical Touch

People who speak this love language thrive on any form of physical touch: hugs, pats on the back, holding hands, and thoughtful touches on the arm, shoulder, or face can all be ways to show excitement, concern, care, and love. Physical presence and accessibility are crucial, while neglect or abuse can be unforgivable and destructive. It's like a dance—a choreography of love expressed through the most primal and intimate form of human connection.

- Offer hugs, cuddles, or physical affection when appropriate and welcomed.

- Hold hands or link arms when walking together.

- Give them gentle touches or caresses to show affection.

- Offer a comforting touch when they are feeling down or stressed.

- Plan activities that involve physical touch, such as couples' massages or dancing.

- Sit close to them and make physical contact, like leaning on their shoulder.

- Offer a supportive touch, like a reassuring pat on the back.

- Initiate playful physical contact, like tickling or playful wrestling.

- Be attentive to their physical comfort and provide warmth or comfort when needed.

- Respect their boundaries and communicate openly about their preferences for physical touch.

Being There and Available for Your Partner in Different Ways

We won't always be able to be there for our partners in the way that we want to be for them, but amidst the ebb and flow of life, there are countless ways we can still paint vibrant strokes of support and love upon the canvas of their existence.

Sometimes, we may find ourselves physically distant from our loved ones, separated by vast oceans or unyielding obligations. In those moments, we must transcend the limitations of mere proximity and bridge the divide with the ethereal threads of connection. We can be present through heartfelt letters that traverse the miles, carrying our words like whispered promises of unwavering devotion. With every stroke of the pen, we inscribe our love on the parchment, creating a tangible testament to our commitment.

When life's storms threaten to engulf our partners in a sea of despair, we can be their steadfast lighthouse, guiding them back to the shores of tranquility. We listen with unwavering attention, our ears attuned to the cadence of their voice and the unspoken nuances of their soul. We offer solace through gentle touches and tender embraces, wrapping them in a cocoon of safety where vulnerability is met with understanding. Our presence becomes a sanctuary, a harbor where they can find respite from the turbulence of life.

In moments of triumph and celebration, we become their most ardent cheerleaders, applauding their every accomplishment with unbridled enthusiasm. We shower them with words of encouragement, fueling their belief in their own remarkable potential. Like master artists, we revel in the brilliance of their achievements and paint a portrait of boundless pride upon their hearts, forever etched in the tapestry of their memories.

But being there for our partners isn't solely about grand gestures or monumental acts of devotion. It's also about the delicate dance of daily life, where the smallest acts can hold profound significance. We can be the steady hand that brews their morning coffee with love, imbuing each sip with warmth and tenderness. We can be the reassuring presence that embraces them after a long day, enveloping them in a cocoon of serenity as the world fades away. We can be the silent companion who holds their hand through life's mundane moments, finding beauty in the ordinary and turning routine into cherished memories.

Ultimately, being there for our partners means cultivating a deep-seated empathy that allows us to anticipate their needs before they even arise. It's about understanding their unspoken desires, their secret hopes, and their hidden fears. It's about embracing their imperfections and loving them unconditionally, as they do for us. It's about being their confidant, their ally, and their safe haven in a world that can often be harsh and unforgiving.

So, even when we can't be there for our partners in the exact way we envision, may we remember that love knows no boundaries. With every word spoken, every touch shared, and every moment cherished, we paint a masterpiece of love, transcending the limitations of time, space, and circumstance. If you are looking for some ideas on how to be there for your partner, here are a few suggestions:

- **Listen actively**: Give your full attention and show genuine interest when they talk.

- **Offer encouragement**: Provide words of encouragement and support when they need it.

- **Show appreciation**: Express gratitude for their efforts and let them know you value them.

- **Be there in tough times**: Offer a shoulder to lean on and provide emotional support during difficult moments.

- **Celebrate their successes**: Acknowledge and celebrate their achievements, no matter how small.

- **Help with tasks**: Offer assistance with everyday tasks or chores to ease their burden.

- **Give compliments**: Offer sincere compliments to boost their confidence and make them feel appreciated.

- **Plan surprises**: Surprise them with small gestures like their favorite meal or a thoughtful gift.

- **Respect their boundaries**: Understand and respect their personal boundaries and give them space when needed.

- **Be a good listener**: Be open and non-judgmental, allowing them to share their thoughts and feelings without fear.

Invest in Yourself and Learn to Love Yourself

In the depths of our souls, where emotions intertwine, and desires bloom, love dances like a delicate flame. It flickers and sways, casting its enchanting glow on the tapestry of our lives. But to truly experience the profound beauty of love, we must first go on a journey of self-discovery and learn to embrace the essence of self-love.

Just as a majestic oak tree draws strength from its roots, our capacity to love others stems from our ability to love ourselves. It is an ethereal connection, a harmonious symphony that resonates within the chambers of our hearts. To love well, we must cultivate a garden of self-appreciation, nurturing the seeds of compassion and acceptance until they blossom into an exquisite bouquet of self-love.

Imagine a serene lake, its surface reflecting the gentle hues of a radiant sunset. In its peaceful depths, the tranquility of self-love resides. When we embark on the path of self-love, we learn to embrace our flaws and imperfections, transforming them into the fertile soil from which our emotional connections with our partners grow. It is in this acceptance of our authentic selves that we find the courage to love others unconditionally.

To love oneself is to embark on a voyage of self-discovery, delving into the recesses of our being to uncover the hidden treasures that lie within. It is in this exploration that we unearth our passions, our dreams, and our desires. By kindling the flame of self-love, we ignite the spark of authenticity, allowing us to bring our truest selves to the sacred dance of love.

In the gentle embrace of self-love, we learn the art of self-care. Just as a painter meticulously tends to their canvas, we tend to the canvas of our souls. We nourish ourselves with compassion, kindness, and forgiveness, recognizing that we are deserving of the love we so freely bestow upon others. Through self-care, we replenish our emotional reservoirs, ensuring that we have an abundance of love to share with our partners.

Self-love is a mirror that reflects the radiance of our inner light. When we gaze into this mirror, we witness the magnificence of our own being, and it is from this place of self-awareness that we can forge genuine connections with our partners. By loving ourselves deeply, we become attuned to our own needs and desires, fostering an environment of mutual understanding and empathy within our relationships.

In the tender embrace of self-love, we become architects of our emotional landscapes. We cultivate the fertile ground of our hearts, sowing seeds of compassion, trust, and vulnerability. As these seeds take root and blossom, our emotional connections with our partners deepen, intertwining our souls in a tapestry of love and intimacy.

To love oneself is to embark on a transformative journey, a pilgrimage of the heart. It is a testament to our innate worthiness and a celebration of our uniqueness and individuality. When we love ourselves well, we become beacons of love, illuminating the path for others to follow. Our emotional connections with our partners flourish as love cascades from the depths of our souls, intertwining and intertwining until it becomes an unbreakable bond.

Small ways to love yourself a little bit louder

- **Embrace your quirks**: Instead of trying to fit into a mold, celebrate your unique qualities and quirks that make you who you are. Embracing these aspects of yourself will help you love and accept yourself more fully.

- **Practice self-compassion**: Treat yourself with kindness and understanding, just as you would a close friend. Remind yourself that it's okay to make mistakes and that you're deserving of forgiveness and compassion.

- **Pamper yourself**: Set aside time for self-care activities that bring you joy and relaxation. Whether it's indulging in a bubble bath, getting a massage, or simply curling up with a good book, prioritize activities that make you feel good.

- **Celebrate your achievements**: Take a moment to acknowledge and celebrate your accomplishments, no matter how small. This could be anything from completing a task at work to learning a new skill. Recognizing your achievements will boost your self-confidence and remind you of your capabilities.

- **Surround yourself with positive influences**: Evaluate the people you spend the most time with and ensure they uplift and support you. Surrounding yourself with positive influences will create an environment that fosters self-love and growth.

- **Practice gratitude**: Cultivate a habit of gratitude by regularly acknowledging the things you're grateful for in your life. This practice will help shift your focus to the positive aspects, allowing you to appreciate and love yourself more deeply.

- **Set boundaries**: Learn to say no when something doesn't align with your values or goals. Setting boundaries will help you prioritize your own needs and prevent feelings of resentment or overwhelm.

- **Engage in self-reflection**: Take time to reflect on your thoughts, emotions, and experiences. Journaling or meditating can help you gain insights into yourself, fostering self-awareness and self-love.

- **Prioritize self-growth**: Invest in personal development activities that align with your interests and aspirations. This could involve taking up a new hobby, attending workshops or seminars, or pursuing further education. The act of investing in yourself will strengthen your self-worth and love.

- **Practice positive affirmations**: Repeat positive affirmations to yourself daily. These affirmations can be personalized statements that remind you of your worth, strengths, and potential. By consistently reinforcing positive beliefs, you'll cultivate a more loving relationship with yourself.

Overcoming Challenges in Intimate Relationships With ADHD

Intimacy, we have learned, is all about opening ourselves up and trusting our partners to come close without hurting us. In the beginning of the chapter, we talked briefly about what intimacy is but didn't really get into the fact that there are different kinds of intimacy. In this section, we take a look at each of them, what they are, and how we can build them with our partners.

Mental Intimacy

Mental intimacy, a profoundly beautiful and vital aspect of our relationships, is the entwining of minds and the shared exploration of thoughts, ideas, dreams, and fears. It's the emotional and intellectual connection that transcends the physical, weaving a fabric of shared understanding and mutual respect. It's the bridge that links two separate consciousnesses, allowing them to converge and create a shared mental landscape.

When we talk about mental intimacy, we talk about the joy of sharing thoughts, the delight in unearthing common interests, the thrill of engaging in stimulating conversations, and the comfort of understanding and being understood. The act of baring our minds to each other, of opening up the labyrinthine corridors of our thoughts, is an act of trust that strengthens the bonds of love.

However, for women with ADHD, achieving this level of mental intimacy can sometimes feel like navigating a maze. The characteristics of ADHD, such as impulsivity, inattentiveness, and hyperactivity, can impact the process of establishing and maintaining mental intimacy.

Impulsivity, a common trait in ADHD, can lead to rushed or thoughtless words, which may inadvertently hurt or confuse their partner. The ability to pause, reflect, and respond thoughtfully is crucial to building mental intimacy. For someone with ADHD, this process may require extra effort and conscious mindfulness.

The inattentiveness characteristic of ADHD can also challenge mental intimacy. Paying consistent attention to a partner's thoughts, dreams, and concerns is a cornerstone of mental intimacy. However, an ADHD mind, often buzzing with a myriad of thoughts, might struggle to focus on a single thread of conversation or to maintain attention to their partner's needs.

Hyperactivity, too, can create hurdles. An overactive mind may leap from thought to thought, making deep, focused conversations a challenge. A partner may feel unheard or overlooked, leading to a sense of disconnect.

Yet, it's important to remember that ADHD also bestows unique strengths. The same impulsivity that can lead to hasty words can also spark spontaneity and creativity in conversations, bringing a unique richness to mental intimacy. Inattentiveness, when managed, can evolve into a broad spectrum of interests and a knack for innovative thinking. Hyperactivity can fuel passionate discussions and an energetic engagement with ideas.

But we, like anyone else, can and do enjoy fulfilling mental intimacy. It may require strategies like mindful listening, practicing patience, and creating structured communication routines, but it's not impossible.

Tips on improving Emotional Emotional Intimacy

- **Open and honest communication**: Encourage open dialogue where both partners feel comfortable expressing their thoughts, feelings, and concerns without judgment or fear of rejection. This can involve sharing personal experiences, discussing relationship dynamics, and addressing any challenges or conflicts that arise.

- **Active listening**: Practice active listening by giving your partner your full attention, maintaining eye contact, and showing genuine interest in what they have to say. Reflecting on their words, asking clarifying questions, and providing thoughtful responses can demonstrate that you value their perspective.

- **Meaningful conversations**: Engage in conversations that go beyond surface-level topics. Discuss shared interests, philosophical ideas, or personal growth. Explore each other's values, beliefs, and life goals. This can create a deeper connection and understanding of each other's inner worlds.

- **Sharing dreams and fears**: Share your dreams, aspirations, and fears with your partner. This vulnerability allows for a deeper level of emotional connection and support. By sharing your hopes and anxieties, you create a space where your partner can do the same, fostering a sense of trust and intimacy.

- **Intellectual stimulation**: Engage in activities that stimulate your minds together. This could involve reading and discussing books, watching thought-provoking movies, attending lectures or workshops, or even engaging in intellectual debates. Such activities can spark interesting conversations and create shared experiences that strengthen mental intimacy.

- **Empathy and respect**: Show empathy and respect for your partner's thoughts, feelings, and perspectives. Seek to understand their point of view, even if you don't agree. Validate their emotions and avoid dismissing or belittling their ideas. This creates a safe space for open and honest communication.

Spiritual Intimacy

Spiritual intimacy is a profound and deeply meaningful connection that goes beyond the physical realm. It is a bond that transcends the tangible and plunges straight into the realm of the soul. When it comes to relationships, spiritual intimacy is an essential foundation that allows us to connect on a higher plane, fostering growth, understanding, and a sense of purpose.

Imagine a cozy evening as you and your partner sit by a crackling fireplace, enveloped in a warm embrace. In this moment, time seems to lose its hold, and you both delve into a deep conversation about the meaning of life, your beliefs, and the universe. As you explore these spiritual depths together, there is a profound sense of connection, a knowing that you are both on a shared journey, supporting and understanding one another on a level beyond words.

Spiritual intimacy involves a shared exploration of values, beliefs, and purpose. It is about nurturing a connection that allows space for individual growth while also fostering a sense of unity. It involves acknowledging and embracing each other's unique spiritual paths, whether they involve religion, mindfulness practices, or a connection with nature.

When partners cultivate spiritual intimacy, they create a safe space for vulnerability, authenticity, and acceptance. This kind of intimacy encourages open communication and a willingness to listen deeply to one another's thoughts, fears, hopes, and dreams. Through this powerful connection, couples gain a deeper understanding of their own spiritual selves and can support one another in their personal growth.

Spiritual intimacy also brings a sense of solace and reassurance during challenging times. When life throws curveballs, it is the spiritual bond that anchors the relationship, providing strength, comfort, and resilience. It reminds partners that they are not alone but rather connected to something greater than themselves, providing a sense of purpose and meaning amidst the chaos of daily life.

Furthermore, spiritual intimacy can enhance other aspects of the relationship, including emotional and physical intimacy. When partners connect on a spiritual level, they gain a deeper understanding of each other's emotional needs, supporting one another in times of emotional vulnerability. This understanding can also extend to physical intimacy, fostering a sense of physical connection that is imbued with love, trust, and respect.

Spiritual intimacy is the thread that weaves through the fabric of a fulfilling and meaningful relationship. It nourishes the connection between us and our partners, allowing them to grow individually and together. By exploring the depths of their spiritual selves, couples can unlock a profound sense of purpose, unity, and unconditional love. It is this sacred bond that ultimately enriches their journey as individuals and their shared experience as partners.

Remember, it is not about adhering to a specific set of beliefs or practices. It is about cultivating a shared understanding, respect, and deep connection that transcends the boundaries of the physical world. Embrace the beauty of spiritual intimacy in your relationship and watch as it becomes a guiding light, illuminating your journey together.

How We Build Spiritual Intimacy

Building spiritual intimacy allows you to foster a bond that transcends the mundane and taps into the profound depths of our souls. It is a shared journey of exploration, understanding, and growth that nurtures both the individual and the relationship. So, how can we actively work towards developing spiritual intimacy? Let's explore six tips that can help you and your partner deepen your spiritual connection and create a sacred space for your love to flourish.

- **Open and Honest Communication**: Spiritual intimacy thrives on open and honest communication. Encourage conversations about your beliefs, values, and spiritual experiences. Share your thoughts, doubts, and aspirations without fear of judgment or rejection. For example, discuss how your individual spiritual practices have shaped your lives and what you hope to gain from them.

- **Engage in Shared Spiritual Practices**: Find ways to engage in shared spiritual practices that resonate with both partners. This can be attending religious services together, meditating in each other's presence, or exploring nature through hikes and walks. By participating in these practices together, you deepen your connection on a spiritual level and create shared memories.

- **Practice Active Listening and Empathy**: Truly listening to your partner's spiritual journey requires empathy and understanding. When your partner opens up about their experiences, make an effort to actively listen without interrupting or judging. Show empathy by acknowledging their emotions and validating their beliefs. This creates a safe and supportive space for genuine connection.

- **Seek Guidance and Learn Together**: Explore spiritual teachings and resources together. Attend workshops, read books, or listen to podcasts that align with both of your interests. Use these opportunities as a gateway to discuss and reflect on your shared spiritual growth. For instance, you might decide to study mindfulness practices together or attend a couples' retreat focused on deepening spiritual connections.

- **Create Rituals and Sacred Spaces**: Rituals can bring a sense of reverence and connection into your relationship. Create simple rituals, such as lighting a candle together before meals or practicing gratitude before bedtime. Additionally, design a sacred space in your home that is dedicated to spiritual reflection, meditation, or prayer. Having a space to retreat to will foster a sense of serenity and intentionality in your spiritual practices.

- **Support Each Other's Spiritual Paths**: It is important to respect and support each other's spiritual paths, even if they differ. Embrace and honor the diversity of beliefs and practices within your relationship. Encourage each other's spiritual growth, attend events that are meaningful to your partner, and engage in open-minded discussions to understand their perspectives. Celebrate the connections that deepen your bond while respecting the individuality that makes your relationship unique.

Physical Intimacy

Physical intimacy is a delicate dance between two souls, an intricate synchronization of bodies and hearts. It is the gentle brush of fingertips across bare skin, the warmth of bodies molded together, and the electric current that courses through us when we make contact with our partners. It is a symphony of sensation, a language spoken without words, and a profound expression of love.

When we speak of physical intimacy, we often think of the rawness of passion and desire. It encompasses the fiery kisses, the ardent embraces, and the intoxicating caresses exchanged between two individuals entwined in an intimate connection. It is the embodiment of our most primal desires: The longing to be seen and cherished by another and the yearning to melt into one another's embrace.

But physical intimacy extends far beyond the realm of passion. It is the tender touches that grace our skin, the comforting presence in a warm embrace, and the shared moments of vulnerability that create a sense of safety and trust within our relationships. It is through physical touch that we communicate our deepest affections, from a gentle stroke along the cheek to a reassuring hand on the back—each gesture conveying more than words ever could.

Within the realm of physical intimacy, there is a language that only lovers truly understand. It is a language whispered through a loving gaze, a soft embrace, or a lingering kiss. It speaks of devotion, passion, and connection, weaving a tapestry that binds two souls together in a dance of vulnerability and intimacy. It is a dance that is unique to each partnership, a language that evolves and deepens over time, creating a profound bond that withstands the test of life's challenges.

Physical intimacy is a vital element that breathes life into our relationships, igniting the flame of love and desire. It affirms our existence, reminding us that we are not alone in this vast universe. It nourishes our souls, providing solace and reassurance in moments of uncertainty. It enhances our emotional connection, reinforcing the foundation of trust and love upon which our relationships are built.

In a world where distractions abound and moments of genuine connection are often fleeting, physical intimacy holds the power to ground us in the present moment. It invites us to surrender ourselves fully to the experience and to embrace the vulnerability that comes with baring our bodies and souls to another. It is a reminder that we are worthy of love, deserving of pleasure, and capable of creating a sense of belonging in the arms of another.

How do we nurture physical intimacy?

Physical intimacy, just like anything else, is worked on:

- **Prioritize quality time**: Make an effort to spend uninterrupted time together, engaging in activities that foster connection and intimacy. This could include going for walks, cooking together, or simply cuddling on the couch.

- **Communicate openly**: Effective communication is crucial for nurturing physical intimacy. Talk openly about your desires, boundaries, and fantasies to ensure both partners feel heard and understood.

- **Explore new experiences**: Trying new things together can reignite the spark in your relationship. Consider attending a couples' dance class, going on a weekend getaway, or experimenting with new hobbies or activities that both partners find enjoyable.

- **Practice non-sexual touch**: Physical intimacy doesn't always have to lead to sexual activity. Simple acts of non-sexual touch, such as holding hands, hugging, or giving massages, can foster a sense of closeness and connection.

- **Create a sensual environment**: Set the mood by creating a sensual and inviting atmosphere in your home. This could involve dimming the lights, playing soft music, or using scented candles or oils to create a relaxing ambiance.

- **Prioritize self-care**: Taking care of your own physical and mental well-being is essential for nurturing intimacy. When you feel good about yourself, you're more likely to feel comfortable and confident in your own skin, which can positively impact your physical intimacy with your partner.

- **Practice active listening**: Show genuine interest in your partner's thoughts, feelings, and desires. By actively listening and responding empathetically, you create a safe space for open and honest communication, which strengthens emotional and physical intimacy.

- **Engage in regular physical activity**: Regular exercise can increase energy levels, boost self-confidence, and improve overall well-being. Engaging in physical activities together, such as going for walks or participating in a sport, can enhance physical intimacy by promoting a sense of shared accomplishment and mutual support.

- **Prioritize touch outside the bedroom**: Physical intimacy should not be limited to the bedroom. Make an effort to incorporate loving touch throughout your day, such as holding hands while walking, giving a gentle touch on the arm, or snuggling together while watching TV.

- **Experiment and be playful**: Embrace a sense of playfulness and explore different ways to connect physically with your partner. This could involve trying new positions, incorporating playful teasing or tickling, or even engaging in fantasy role-playing to keep the excitement alive. Remember, the key is to always prioritize consent and respect each other's boundaries.

A final few things to remember about physical intimacy

- **Consent is essential**: Always prioritize consent and ensure that both partners are comfortable and enthusiastic about engaging in physical intimacy.

- **It's a journey, not a destination**: Physical intimacy is not solely focused on the end result but rather the journey of connection, exploration, and pleasure that you share with your partner.

- **Communication is key**: Open and honest communication is vital for understanding each other's desires, boundaries, and needs. Regularly check in with your partner and create a safe space for dialogue.

- **It's not just about sex**: Physical intimacy encompasses a wide range of activities beyond sexual intercourse. Embrace and appreciate the various forms of physical connection that can bring you closer together.

- **It's unique for every couple**: Each couple has their own preferences, desires, and comfort levels when it comes to physical intimacy. Embrace and celebrate the uniqueness of your connection with your partner.

- **It requires vulnerability**: Being vulnerable and open with your partner allows for a deeper and more meaningful physical connection. Trust and emotional intimacy are often intertwined with physical intimacy.

- **It's a two-way street**: Physical intimacy should be a mutually enjoyable experience. Both partners should actively participate, listen to each other's needs, and prioritize each other's pleasure.

- **It can evolve and change**: Physical intimacy can evolve and change throughout a relationship. Be open to exploring new experiences and adapting to each other's changing desires and preferences.

- **It's not always perfect**: Physical intimacy, like any aspect of a relationship, can have its ups and downs. It's important to be patient, understanding, and supportive of each other, especially during challenging times.

- **It's about connection and love**: Physical intimacy is a powerful way to express love, affection, and connection with your partner. Embrace the emotional and physical bond that it can create, fostering a deeper connection in your relationship.

Emotional Intimacy

Emotional intimacy is a profound connection that transcends the physical realm, weaving together the hearts and minds of two individuals. It is a sacred space where vulnerability is embraced, trust is nurtured, and understanding is cultivated. Like a delicate dance, it requires both partners to be fully present, engaged, and willing to explore the depths of their emotions.

In this intimacy, words become a symphony of emotions, painting vivid pictures of our innermost thoughts and desires. It is a language that surpasses mere conversation, delving into the realm of empathy and compassion. Here, we speak not only with our voices but also with our eyes, our touch, and our presence. It is a connection that allows us to truly see and be seen, to understand and be understood.

Within emotional intimacy, walls are dismantled, and masks are shed. It is a space that invites raw authenticity, where we can share our fears, hopes, and dreams without fear of judgment. In these moments, we find solace in knowing that our partners accept us for who we are, our imperfections and all. It is a sanctuary where vulnerability is not a weakness but rather a source of strength, forging a bond that withstands the tests of time.

Emotional intimacy matters because it is the lifeblood of a healthy and fulfilling relationship. It is the foundation upon which trust is built, allowing love to flourish and grow. Without it, relationships become stagnant, lacking the depth and richness that come from truly knowing one another.

When emotional intimacy thrives, conflicts become opportunities for growth and understanding. Partners can navigate the ebbs and flows of life together, finding solace in each other's arms. It is a safe haven where we can seek refuge from the storms of the outside world, knowing that our partner's love and support will always be there.

Moreover, emotional intimacy is a catalyst for personal growth. Through the mirror of our partners, we gain insights into our own emotions, beliefs, and patterns. We learn to confront our fears and insecurities, allowing them to be transformed into sources of strength.

It is within this intimate connection that we find the courage to become the best versions of ourselves.

Yet emotional intimacy is not without its challenges. It requires effort, patience, and a willingness to explore the depths of our own emotions. It demands open-hearted communication, active listening, and a genuine curiosity to understand our partner's inner world. It necessitates setting aside distractions, carving out quality time, and prioritizing the sacred bond we share.

In the realm of emotional intimacy, we discover that love is not merely a noun but a verb. It is a continuous journey of discovery, growth, and connection. It is a dance of emotions where partners move in harmony, supporting and uplifting one another.

Tips on creating emotional intimacy

Achieving emotional intimacy requires effort; it's not just something that's going to happen on its own. Let's take a look at some strategies we can employ to achieve this.

Don't depend on one person for all your emotional needs: Relying solely on our partners to fulfill all our emotional needs can put a tremendous strain on the relationship. By diversifying our sources of support, we empower ourselves and foster personal growth. It also reduces the burden on our partners, allowing them to be more present and engaged.

Imagine having a close-knit group of friends who offer different perspectives and a network of support. Maintaining a strong social circle can provide varied emotional outlets, preventing one person from becoming overwhelmed or feeling suffocated. Additionally, engaging in hobbies, joining support groups, or seeking professional therapy can offer additional avenues for emotional expression. By taking the initiative to expand our support system, we become less dependent on our partners and create a more balanced dynamic in our relationship. This freedom allows each individual to thrive, enhancing the overall emotional intimacy as both partners bring their unique experiences and interests to the connection.

Leave your comfort zone and take accountability: Emotional intimacy blossoms when we take accountability for our emotions and are willing to step outside our comfort zones. It requires vulnerability, honesty, and a willingness to engage in open and compassionate communication. By addressing our own emotional barriers, we create a safe space for our partners to do the same. Let's consider a couple who have difficulty expressing their insecurities. By individually acknowledging their fears and sharing them with their partner, they can overcome the obstacles hindering emotional intimacy. This act of vulnerability opens the door for empathetic understanding and encourages the other partner to reciprocate, deepening the emotional connection.

Engaging in new experiences together is another powerful way to foster emotional intimacy. By exploring unfamiliar terrain, such as traveling to a new destination or trying a new activity, couples create shared memories and establish a secure space to support each other in times of uncertainty. Stepping outside our comfort zones hand in hand strengthens the bond, allowing for emotional growth and resilience as a couple.

Create a Safe Space for Open Communication: One crucial aspect of developing emotional intimacy is creating a safe and judgment-free space for open communication. This means actively listening to your partner, being receptive to their emotions, and providing support without judgment or criticism. Encouraging your partner to express their thoughts and feelings freely, even if they differ from your own, fosters trust and mutual understanding. To create this safe space, practice active listening techniques, such as maintaining eye contact, reflecting back on what your partner has said, and showing empathy. By validating their emotions, even if you don't necessarily agree, you demonstrate respect and reinforce the bond of emotional intimacy.

Practice Patience and Understanding: Building emotional intimacy takes time and patience. It involves understanding that each partner has their own unique journey and pace. It's essential to respect and acknowledge that individuals may have different comfort levels when it comes to emotional vulnerability. Allow your partner the space to open up at their own pace, without pressure or expectations. Be patient and understanding when they share their emotions, even if it takes longer than you anticipated. Rushing the process may cause your partner to withdraw or feel overwhelmed.

By practicing patience, you show your commitment to nurturing the emotional bond, allowing it to grow naturally and authentically. Remember, true emotional intimacy is built on trust and a deep understanding of one another, which can develop most effectively when given room to flourish.

Avoid Rushing the Process. Emotional intimacy is not something that can be forced or rushed. It requires a willingness to be present and invest in the development of the relationship. Avoid placing unrealistic expectations on yourself or your partner to achieve a certain level of emotional intimacy within a specific timeframe. Allow the relationship to unfold naturally, adapting to the ebb and flow of emotions. Rushing the process may result in superficial connections or a lack of trust. Instead, focus on engaging in meaningful conversations, being vulnerable, and embracing vulnerability together.

Remember, emotional intimacy is a continuous journey that evolves over time. By savoring the small moments of connection, demonstrating patience, and avoiding the pressure to reach arbitrary milestones, you create an environment where emotional intimacy can flourish organically.

Building Trust and Vulnerability in Romantic Partnerships

Amber and Ethan had been in a relationship for several years, but something always felt missing. Amber, who has ADHD, struggled with opening up and being vulnerable with Ethan. She feared that her ADHD-related challenges would make her appear unreliable or incapable of maintaining a deep emotional connection. It wasn't until a pivotal moment of honesty and understanding that they began to build trust and vulnerability, transforming their relationship into a stronger and more intimate bond.

Amber's fear of being judged and misunderstood due to her ADHD made it difficult for her to fully open up to Ethan. She had always felt the need to hide her struggles, worried that they would be seen as weaknesses or flaws. This fear created a barrier between them, preventing them from truly connecting on a deeper level.

One evening, as they sat together on the couch, Amber mustered up the courage to share her deepest insecurities and fears related to her ADHD. She expressed her concerns about being unreliable, forgetful, and easily distracted. To her surprise, Ethan listened attentively, his eyes filled with empathy and understanding.

Instead of dismissing her concerns or downplaying her struggles, Ethan validated Amber's feelings. He reassured her that he saw beyond her ADHD and loved her for who she was—challenges and all. He shared his own vulnerabilities, explaining that everyone has their own unique struggles and that he was committed to supporting her through hers.

This pivotal moment of honesty and understanding marked the beginning of a new chapter in their relationship. Amber realized that she didn't have to face her ADHD alone; she had a partner who was willing to stand by her side and help her navigate the challenges. Ethan's acceptance and support created a safe space for Amber to be vulnerable without fear of judgment.

As time went on, Amber and Ethan actively worked on building trust and vulnerability in their relationship. They established open lines of communication, regularly checking in with each other about their needs and concerns. They developed strategies together to manage ADHD-related difficulties, such as creating routines and setting reminders.

Through their shared efforts, their bond grew stronger and more intimate. Amber discovered that vulnerability wasn't a weakness but rather a strength that allowed her to deepen her connection with Ethan. She learned to embrace her ADHD as a part of her identity, knowing that it didn't define her worth or her ability to love and be loved.

Their journey wasn't without its challenges, of course. There were times when Amber's ADHD symptoms caused misunderstandings or frustrations. However, their foundation of trust and vulnerability allowed them to navigate these obstacles with compassion and patience.

In the end, Amber and Ethan's relationship became a testament to the power of building trust and vulnerability. By embracing their true selves and accepting each other's imperfections, they created a love that was resilient, understanding, and deeply fulfilling.

How to Make Space for Trust and Vulnerability in Relationships

Building trust and fostering vulnerability in relationships is akin to nurturing a garden—it requires time, patience, and a lot of tender care. Let's delve into eight ways we can cultivate this beautiful garden.

Open Communication: Imagine you're on a road trip with a friend. If you don't communicate about your destination, you'll end up lost or, worse, in a disagreement. Similarly, relationships thrive on open, honest, and clear communication. Discuss your feelings, fears, dreams, and expectations. Share that story about your childhood that still makes you laugh, or express why a certain comment hurts your feelings. It's like giving someone a map to your heart.

Consistent Actions: Trust is built incrementally, much like a sandcastle by the sea. Each grain of sand represents a promise kept, a secret respected, or a supportive gesture. Over time, these small actions create a solid foundation of trust. For instance, if you say you'll be there for someone, ensure you show up when they need you. Consistency in your actions is key:

- **Active Listening**: Imagine a friend sharing a painful experience, and instead of providing comfort, you're busy formulating your response. Active listening goes beyond hearing words. It involves understanding, responding, and remembering. By doing this, you're essentially saying, "I see you, I hear you, and what you're saying matters to me."

- **Empathy and Understanding**: Trust blossoms when you demonstrate empathy. Imagine your partner having a hard day at work. Rather than offering solutions, simply saying, "That sounds tough; I'm here for you," can provide solace. Understanding doesn't always mean solving problems; sometimes, it's just about providing emotional support.

- **Acceptance**: Everyone has quirks, makes mistakes, and carries baggage. Acceptance is like inviting someone into a warm, cozy home, reassuring them they're loved and respected, imperfections and all. For example, if your friend is terrified of spiders, instead of teasing them, help them feel secure when they encounter one.

- **Transparency**: Trust is like a window. When it's clean and clear, you can see the other person's intentions and feelings. But a crack in the glass can create mistrust. Be transparent about your thoughts and emotions. If something bothers you, express it gently and honestly.

- **Patience**: Building trust and vulnerability doesn't happen overnight. It's similar to growing a tree from a tiny seed—it requires time, care, and patience. For instance, if your partner has been hurt in the past, they might need time to open up. Be patient and give them the space they need.

- **Respect and Boundaries**: Trust entails respecting each other's boundaries. If your friend confides in you about a personal matter and asks you not to share it with anyone, respect their request. Like a beautiful garden with well-defined paths, a relationship needs boundaries to thrive.

By continuing to tend to our gardens with open communication, consistency, active listening, empathy, acceptance, transparency, patience, and respect, we can cultivate spaces where trust blooms and vulnerability feels safe. Like any gardening endeavor, there will be challenges; rainy days, weeds, and pests. But remember, these challenges are necessary.

Love Languages and ADHD

Imagine that love languages are like different musical instruments in an orchestra. Each instrument has its own unique sound and way of expressing melodies, just as each love language has its own distinct way of expressing and receiving love:

- **Words of Affirmation—the Violin**: Words of affirmation are like the sweet, soaring melodies of a violin. Just as the violin's delicate notes can evoke emotions and bring joy, words of affirmation have the power to uplift and inspire. However, when ADHD is involved, it's like the violinist occasionally struggles to maintain a steady rhythm or forgets some of the notes. The ability to consistently provide verbal affirmations and compliments might be affected by difficulties with attention and focus.

- **Acts of Service—the Piano**: Acts of Service are like the harmonious chords of a piano. Similar to how the piano keys are played with purpose and precision, acts of service involve doing helpful actions and tasks for your loved one. With ADHD in the mix, it can be like having a few sticky piano keys that don't always respond as intended. Partners with ADHD may struggle with organization and time management, making it challenging to consistently follow through on acts of service.

- **Receiving Gifts—the Trumpet**: Receiving gifts is like the bold and vibrant sound of a trumpet. Just as the trumpet's powerful notes can leave a lasting impact, receiving gifts symbolizes the thoughtfulness and significance behind a tangible expression of love. ADHD can be like having a trumpet player who occasionally plays off-key. Impulsivity and forgetfulness might affect the ability to consider the importance and meaning behind gift-giving.

- **Quality Time—the Flute**: Quality Time is like the gentle and soothing melody of a flute. Just as the flute's serene notes create an atmosphere of intimacy, quality time involves undivided attention and shared experiences. But with ADHD, it's like occasionally having a flutist who struggles to maintain focus or gets lost in their thoughts. Distraction, restlessness, and difficulty with time management can make it challenging for individuals with ADHD to provide their partner with the focused, uninterrupted time they desire.

- **Physical Touch—the Drum Set**: Physical Touch is akin to the rhythmic beats of a drum set. Just as the drums provide a sense of connection and energy, physical touch represents non-sexual affection and closeness. Sometimes with ADHD, though, it's like having a drummer who sometimes plays too softly or too loudly. Sensory sensitivity and hyperactivity can influence how individuals with ADHD experience physical touch, ranging from a heightened need for stimulation to finding it overwhelming or uncomfortable.

Adapting Love Languages to Accommodate These Challenges

Adapting love languages to accommodate ADHD-related challenges requires open communication, empathy, and a willingness to find mutually beneficial solutions. Each relationship is unique, so it's important to tailor these strategies to your specific circumstances and the needs of both partners. In the meantime, here are some strategies you can try:

- **Words of Affirmation**: Utilize written notes or text messages: Instead of relying solely on verbal affirmations, consider expressing your love and appreciation through written notes or text messages. This allows the person with ADHD to read and revisit the messages at their own pace.

- **Acts of Service**: Create visual reminders: Use visual cues, such as sticky notes or digital reminders, to help individuals with ADHD remember tasks or commitments. This can help them follow through on acts of service more consistently.

- **Receiving Gifts**: Plan ahead and set reminders: If gift-giving is important, work together to create a calendar or reminder system to help the person with ADHD remember special occasions. This way, they can plan ahead and select meaningful gifts instead of relying on last-minute impulses.

- **Quality Time**: Establish structured routines: Establishing structured routines can help individuals with ADHD manage their time and be more present during quality time. Plan specific activities or dedicated periods for uninterrupted quality time to minimize distractions.

- **Physical Touch**: Communicate and respect boundaries—people with ADHD may have sensory sensitivities or preferences regarding physical touch. It's important to have open communication and respect their boundaries. Discuss what types of touch are comfortable and enjoyable for both partners.

Additionally, there are some general strategies that can be helpful for accommodating ADHD-related challenges in any love language:

- o **Practice listening**: When your partner with ADHD is expressing their love language, make a conscious effort to listen actively and attentively. This can help minimize misunderstandings and strengthen communication.

- o **Seek professional support**: Consider involving a therapist or counselor who specializes in ADHD. They can provide guidance, coping strategies, and tools tailored to your specific relationship dynamics.

- o **Practice patience and understanding**: ADHD-related challenges can create frustrations and misunderstandings in relationships. Cultivate patience and understanding, recognizing that ADHD is a neurodevelopmental condition and not a personal failing.

- o **Collaborate and problem-solve together**: Work as a team to identify specific challenges and find creative solutions that accommodate both partners' needs. Collaboration and problem-solving can help build stronger and more supportive relationships.

Rejection Sensitivity

Reject sensitivity, also known as rejection sensitivity dysphoria (RSD), is a common trait associated with ADHD. It refers to an intense emotional response to perceived or actual rejection, criticism, or disapproval from others. Those of us with ADHD who experience rejection sensitivity often have heightened sensitivity to social cues and are more prone to interpret neutral or ambiguous situations as signs of rejection or failure.

In the context of relationships, rejection sensitivity can have a significant impact on emotional connections. Sometimes, we constantly worry about being rejected or abandoned by our partner, even in the absence of concrete evidence or logical reasons for such concerns. This hypersensitivity can lead to a heightened fear of rejection, which can manifest as constant questioning of the partner's love and commitment, seeking reassurance excessively, or becoming overly defensive in response to perceived criticism.

This constant fear of rejection can create a cycle of insecurity and anxiety in relationships. You become overly vigilant for signs of rejection, which can strain your emotional connection with your partner. You may struggle to trust your partner's affection and loyalty, always doubting their intentions. This can lead to frequent conflicts, misunderstandings, and emotional distance.

Additionally, rejection sensitivity can have a profound impact on trust within relationships. Individuals with ADHD and high rejection sensitivity may find it challenging to trust others fully, as they are always on high alert for signs of rejection or betrayal. They may have a pervasive fear of being hurt, which can make it difficult for them to open up emotionally or be vulnerable in their relationships. This lack of trust can impede the development of deep emotional connections and intimacy.

Tips for learning to deal with rejection sensitivity.

Increase self-awareness: Developing self-awareness is crucial in managing rejection sensitivity. Take the time to recognize and understand your own patterns of thinking and emotional responses when it comes to perceived rejection. Pay attention to the situations or triggers that tend to provoke intense feelings of rejection. For example, you may notice that you feel particularly sensitive when your partner is busy or preoccupied with something else. By identifying these patterns, you can start to challenge and reframe your thoughts.

When you notice yourself feeling rejected because your partner is busy, remind yourself that their busyness is not a reflection of their love or commitment to you. Recognize that they have other responsibilities and that it doesn't mean they don't care about you.

Challenge Negative Thoughts: Rejection sensitivity often involves negative interpretations and assumptions about others' intentions or behaviors. Practice challenging these negative thoughts and replacing them with more balanced and realistic ones. Consider alternative explanations for the situation that don't involve rejection or failure. This can help you regain a more accurate perspective and reduce the intensity of emotional reactions.

Instead of immediately assuming that your partner's criticism means they don't value you, consider that they may have had a challenging day, and their comment was not intended as a personal attack. Remind yourself that everyone has ups and downs, and it doesn't necessarily reflect on your worth.

Communicate Openly: Effective communication is essential in addressing rejection sensitivity within relationships. Talk openly with your partner about your feelings and fears related to rejection. Share your experiences and educate them about how rejection sensitivity impacts you. This can help your partner better understand your needs and provide reassurance when you're feeling vulnerable. It's important to create a safe space where both partners can express their thoughts and emotions without judgment.

Sit down with your partner and have an honest conversation about your reject sensitivity. Explain that sometimes you may become overly sensitive to perceived rejection and that it's not a reflection of their actions. Share specific examples to help them understand what triggers your sensitivity and how they can support you during those times.

Remember, working on rejection sensitivity is a process that takes time and practice. Be patient with yourself and celebrate small achievements along the way.

ADHD and Self-Care

Self-care involves intentionally engaging in activities that promote physical, mental, and emotional health. It's about taking time for yourself to recharge, reduce stress, and nurture your overall well-being. When practiced together with your partner, it can strengthen your relationship and provide mutual support. Here are some self-care practices you can explore:

- **Mindfulness or Meditation**: Mindfulness involves bringing your attention to the present moment without judgment. It can help individuals with ADHD and their partners cultivate greater awareness, reduce stress, and enhance emotional resilience. You can engage in mindfulness or meditation practices together, such as guided meditations or mindful breathing exercises. This can create a peaceful and calming atmosphere, fostering a sense of connection and relaxation.

- **Physical Activity**: Engaging in physical activity is not only beneficial for your physical health but also for managing ADHD symptoms and promoting overall well-being. Explore different physical activities with your partner, such as going for walks or hikes, practicing yoga together, or participating in a sport you both enjoy. Exercise releases endorphins, which can improve mood and reduce stress, creating a positive and energizing experience for both of you.

- **Quality Time**: Carving out quality time to spend together as a couple is an essential form of self-care. It allows you to connect, bond, and nurture your relationship. Plan activities that you both enjoy and that help you unwind and relax. It could be something as simple as cooking a meal together, having a movie night, or going on a date. Quality time provides an opportunity to escape the demands of daily life and focus on nurturing your emotional connection.

- **Establishing Boundaries**: Setting boundaries is a crucial aspect of self-care, as it helps protect your emotional well-being and maintain a healthy balance in your relationships. Discuss and establish boundaries with your partner, such as designating alone time for each of you to engage in activities you enjoy independently. This can provide a sense of autonomy and personal space while still maintaining a strong partnership. Respecting each other's boundaries fosters trust, understanding, and overall relationship satisfaction.

- **Practicing Self-Compassion**: Self-compassion involves treating yourself with kindness, understanding, and acceptance. It's about acknowledging your strengths and imperfections without self-judgment. Individuals with ADHD often face challenges and may experience self-criticism. By practicing self-compassion, you can cultivate a more positive and nurturing relationship with yourself. Encourage your partner to engage in self-compassion practices as well, fostering a supportive and compassionate environment within your relationship.

Chapter 7:

Support Systems and Relationships

In those moments when Ashley felt overwhelmed by the challenges of ADHD, she found solace and strength in the power of community and supportive relationships. As she navigated the ups and downs of her journey, she discovered the transformative impact of surrounding herself with understanding friends, family, and professionals who uplifted and supported her. This is a story of how community and strong relationships became the pillars of her resilience and growth.

Ashley often found herself sitting in her university library, poring over textbooks on psychology. She was a hardworking student, dedicated to her studies, but there were times when she felt like she was battling a storm inside her mind. The words on the pages would dance before her eyes, refusing to settle into coherent thoughts. The constant whirlwind of distractions was a battle she fought daily, a hallmark of her ADHD.

For a long time, Ashley felt isolated, as though she were sailing a turbulent sea alone. She wrestled with the feeling that nobody could understand the intensity of her struggles. The relentless cycle of focus, distraction, and self-reprimand left her exhausted and disheartened.

But everything changed one day when she stumbled upon an ADHD support group on campus. This group, composed of students like her and empathetic faculty members, became her sanctuary. It was here that she met Tom, a senior who had learned to harness his ADHD into a powerful tool of creativity and innovation. There was also Professor Davis, a compassionate psychologist who had spent her career researching ADHD and its impacts on young adults.

In this company, Ashley no longer felt alone. She found comfort in shared experiences and camaraderie in shared challenges. The group became her safe haven, where she could openly express her frustrations without fear of judgment. They laughed together, cried together, and, more importantly, learned together. It was in this group that Ashley first heard the term "neurodiversity"—a term that reframed her perception of ADHD from a disability to a different, valuable way of thinking.

With the encouragement of her newfound support system, Ashley began to see her ADHD not as a debilitating disorder but as a unique aspect of her identity. She learned strategies to manage her symptoms, sure, but she also started to appreciate the creativity and originality that her ADHD brought to her studies.

Her relationship with her family, too, transformed. Once frustrated by her unpredictable focus and energy, they now began to understand and empathize with her struggles. They provided a steadfast pillar of support, cheering her on as she turned her challenges into strengths.

There were still times when Ashley felt overwhelmed when the words on the pages blurred into an indecipherable mess. But now she had a community to turn to. She had Tom's inspiring stories, Professor Davis' wise guidance, and her family's unwavering support. They were her lighthouse in the storm, guiding her through the tumultuous waves.

This was the power of community and supportive relationships—they provided Ashley not only with the tools to manage her ADHD but also a new lens through which to view herself. She was not broken, she realized, but simply different. And in her differences lay her strength. This is a story of how community and strong relationships became the pillars of her resilience and growth.

Building Effective Communication With Our Loved Ones

When it comes to educating our loved ones about our struggles and challenges with ADHD, effective communication is key. It's important to have open and honest conversations that allow us to share our experiences and help them understand what we're going through.

First and foremost, it's crucial to approach these conversations with empathy and understanding. Remember that our loved ones may not have a full grasp of what ADHD entails, so patience is essential. Start by expressing your desire to educate them about your experiences and how ADHD impacts your daily life.

One effective way to communicate is by sharing personal anecdotes or stories that illustrate specific challenges you face due to ADHD. By providing real-life examples, you can help your loved ones visualize and empathize with your struggles. For instance, you could talk about how difficulty with focus and organization makes it challenging to complete tasks or meet deadlines.

It's also important to explain that ADHD is not just about being easily distracted or forgetful. Help them understand that it's a neurodevelopmental disorder that affects various aspects of your life, including emotions, relationships, and self-esteem. Share information from reputable sources or recommend books and articles that provide a deeper understanding of ADHD.

Active listening is another crucial aspect of effective communication. Encourage your loved ones to ask questions and express their thoughts and concerns. By actively listening to their perspective, you can address any misconceptions or fears they may have. This creates a space for dialogue and mutual understanding.

In addition to sharing your struggles, it's equally important to communicate your needs and preferences. Let your loved ones know what kind of support and accommodations you find helpful. This could include setting reminders, creating structured routines, or finding alternative ways to communicate effectively.

Lastly, emphasize that ADHD is a part of who you are, but it doesn't define you entirely. Highlight your strengths and achievements, showcasing that ADHD can also bring unique qualities and perspectives. By focusing on the positive aspects, you can help your loved ones see beyond the challenges and appreciate the whole person you are.

Remember, building effective communication takes time and effort. Be patient with your loved ones as they learn and adjust their understanding. By fostering open and ongoing conversations, you can create a supportive environment where everyone feels heard and understood.

The Role of Therapy

Couples therapy, individual therapy, or family therapy can be incredibly beneficial in managing ADHD-related challenges. These therapeutic approaches provide a supportive and structured environment where individuals and couples can learn effective strategies, improve communication, and develop coping mechanisms.

In couples therapy, you and your partner can gain a deeper understanding of how ADHD impacts their relationship dynamics. The therapist can help identify specific challenges related to ADHD, such as difficulties with organization, time management, or impulsivity. By addressing these challenges together, couples can work towards finding practical solutions and developing strategies that support both partners.

Individual therapy, on the other hand, focuses on the needs of the person with ADHD. It provides a safe space for you to explore the emotional and psychological impact of ADHD on your daily life. The therapist can help individuals develop self-awareness, manage emotions, and build self-esteem. They can also assist in developing personalized strategies to improve focus, organization, and time management skills.

Family therapy involves the participation of the entire family unit. It can be particularly helpful when ADHD affects multiple family members. The therapist can educate the family about ADHD, its symptoms, and its impact on relationships. They can facilitate open and honest communication, helping family members understand and support each other. Family therapy can also assist in establishing routines, setting boundaries, and implementing strategies that benefit everyone involved.

Therapy provides a structured and supportive environment where you can learn effective coping mechanisms, improve communication skills, and develop strategies to manage ADHD-related challenges. Therapists can offer guidance, education, and practical tools tailored to the unique needs of each individual or couple.

Creating a Supportive Environment

Thriving as a woman with ADHD is as much about having a strong support system as it is about creating a supportive environment for yourself. It is really important to look at your life and find ways, however big or small, to make it as easy as possible. Here are a few great starting places for you:

Establishing a Morning Routine

Imagine starting your day with a well-defined routine. You can set up a consistent sequence of tasks that helps you ease into the day. For instance, you might wake up at the same time each morning, have a nutritious breakfast, engage in a short exercise routine, and then spend a few minutes practicing mindfulness or meditation. Following a structured morning routine can provide a sense of stability and set a positive tone for the rest of the day.

Designating a Distraction-Free Workspace

Picture a workspace that fosters focus and productivity. You can create this by selecting a specific area in your home or office where you can work without distractions. Remove unnecessary clutter and organize your materials in a way that helps you stay organized. Consider using noise-cancelling headphones or playing soft instrumental music to minimize external distractions. Additionally, using tools like time-blocking or setting specific goals for each work session can help you maintain focus and manage your time effectively.

Creating Regular Breaks and Transition Times

Think about incorporating regular breaks and transition times into your schedule. As an ADHD woman, it's essential to recognize that your attention span may fluctuate throughout the day. Allow yourself short breaks between tasks to recharge and refocus. These breaks could include stretching, going for a short walk, or engaging in a brief mindfulness exercise. Additionally, incorporating transition times between activities can help you mentally shift gears and prepare for the next task.

Remember, you don't have to navigate this journey all on your own; help, if you look hard and long enough, is always right around the corner. In the next chapter, we navigate the journey of parenthood with ADHD, so go give yourself a break, make a cup of tea, and come back refreshed so that we can navigate this together.

Chapter 8:

Parenting With ADHD

Imagine this: a group of women sitting together, sharing stories about their experiences as parents. They laugh, they nod in agreement, and they exchange knowing glances. As the conversation unfolds, one common thread emerges: The pursuit of being the "perfect parent." Each woman in the circle has her own insecurities and doubts, but one story stands out—a tale of a mother with ADHD navigating the challenges and triumphs of parenting. Meet Samantha, a vibrant and passionate woman who exudes love and warmth. Her children, Emily and Ben, are her pride and joy. But it hasn't always been an easy journey for Samantha. She was diagnosed with ADHD in her late twenties, after years of feeling different and struggling to keep up with the demands of everyday life.

Samantha vividly recalls the day she received her diagnosis. It was as if a fog had lifted, and suddenly, everything made sense. She finally had a name for the challenges she faced—difficulties with organization, forgetfulness, and easily becoming overwhelmed. Armed with this newfound knowledge, Samantha embarked on a mission to understand how her ADHD affected her role as a mother.

In the early years of motherhood, Samantha often felt overwhelmed and judged by society's expectations. She read countless parenting books and tried to implement their advice, but it seemed like an impossible task. She would forget important school events, lose track of time, and struggle with maintaining a consistent routine. The guilt would eat at her as she questioned whether she was failing her children.

One day, when Emily was six years old, she came home from school in tears. Samantha's heart sank as she listened to her daughter's words, "Mommy, why are you always so forgetful? Why can't you be like other moms?" Those words pierced Samantha's soul, and in that moment, she resolved to turn things around.

Samantha embarked on a journey of self-discovery and self-acceptance. She attended support groups for parents with ADHD, where she found solace in connecting with others who understood her struggles. Through these shared experiences, she realized that she was not alone.

With newfound determination and a fresh perspective, Samantha began implementing strategies tailored to her ADHD. She created visual schedules for her children with colorful charts and reminders that helped everyone stay on track. She established daily routines that provided structure and stability, soothing the chaos that ADHD often brought into their lives.

But it wasn't just about finding practical solutions—Samantha also learned to embrace her unique strengths as an ADHD parent. Her creativity and spontaneity brought a sense of joy and adventure to her children's lives. She encouraged their imaginations to soar, engaging in impromptu dance parties and creating fantastical stories that sparked their curiosity.

Samantha's journey as a mother with ADHD has taught her the importance of self-compassion and resilience. She's learned to celebrate the small victories and forgive herself for the occasional missteps. Through her unwavering love and dedication, she has shown Emily and Ben that being different is a gift, one that can bring immense love and joy into their lives.

As Samantha shares her story with the group of women, their eyes well up with tears. They see themselves reflected in her struggles, but more importantly, they see hope. They realize that perfection is an unattainable myth and that embracing their unique journeys as ADHD mothers is what truly matters.

In that moment, a powerful bond forms among these women—a sisterhood of support and understanding. They continue to exchange stories, laughter, and tears, knowing that they are not alone on this challenging yet beautiful path of parenting with ADHD.

Managing the Unique Challenges of Parenting With ADHD

Living with ADHD is already a challenge in itself—trying to navigate the complexities of parenthood with ADHD can feel like an uphill battle. Parents with ADHD often face unique obstacles that require strength, resilience, and a deep understanding of their condition.

One of the primary challenges of being a parent with ADHD is maintaining consistency and structure. ADHD can make it difficult to stick to routines, stay organized, and follow through on tasks. For children who thrive on predictability and stability, this inconsistency can be confusing and unsettling. We may find ourselves grappling with the constant struggle to establish and maintain a sense of order in our children's lives.

Time management presents another significant hurdle. ADHD can affect our perception of time, making it challenging to estimate how long tasks will take or manage schedules effectively. This can result in missed appointments, forgotten obligations, and a constant feeling of being rushed or overwhelmed. When raising children who have their own schedules and demands, this time-related difficulty can amplify stress and strain on both the parent and the child.

Let's not forget about that impulsivity that we have been talking about throughout the book. ADHD may leave you reacting impulsively to your children's behavior, sometimes resorting to inconsistent discipline, or giving in to demands without considering the long-term consequences. These impulsive reactions can lead to confusion and frustration for both you and the child because the lines of boundaries and expectations may become blurred.

Parental self-care is crucial for any parent, but it takes on even greater importance when dealing with ADHD because it can be physically and mentally exhausting, as the brain constantly seeks stimulation and struggles with maintaining focus. You need to prioritize self-care activities to recharge and manage your symptoms effectively.

But let's not forget that, despite these challenges, parents with ADHD also possess unique strengths that can positively influence their parenting. Creativity, spontaneity, and a sense of playfulness can infuse joy and excitement into family life. Your ability to think outside the box and approach problems from different angles can lead to innovative solutions and novel experiences for your children.

Recognizing and addressing the challenges of parenting with ADHD requires a multifaceted approach. Maybe professional support shouldn't be out of the question. Building a strong support network of understanding friends, family members, or other parents with ADHD can offer a safe space for sharing experiences and exchanging advice. But above all, practicing self-compassion and embracing your unique journey as a parent with ADHD is crucial. Parenting is a continuous learning process for everyone, and acknowledging that mistakes will happen is part of the growth. By focusing on strengths, finding effective strategies, and nurturing a loving and supportive environment, you can navigate the challenges of parenting while fostering deep connections and creating a fulfilling family life.

Parenting Styles

Parenting is a complex and individual journey that varies from family to family. It is important to recognize that there is no one-size-fits-all approach to raising children, as each child and parent is unique and requires different forms of guidance and support. What works for one family may not work for another, and it is crucial to be open-minded and adaptable in our parenting styles. Understanding and respecting the individual needs that we have is key to creating a nurturing and supportive environment for their growth and development.

So, there are four primary parenting styles: authoritative, permissive, uninvolved, and authoritarian. Each has its own unique strengths and weaknesses, and understanding them can empower us to foster a positive and nurturing home environment.

Authoritative parenting is characterized by a balance of rule enforcement and emotional responsiveness. It's a style where you set clear rules but also engage in open and empathetic communication with your children. Organization and consistency might be challenging, but you can adapt by using tools like visual reminders, alarms, or scheduling apps to help maintain consistency. You can also use their experiences with ADHD to empathize with their child's struggles, encouraging open conversations and developing coping strategies together.

Permissive Parenting is a style marked by leniency. These parents are responsive and loving but set few boundaries. If you are a parent with ADHD, this style might naturally align with your spontaneous and flexible nature. But it's crucial to ensure a stable structure for children. You can adapt this style by setting a few essential rules and creating a loose but consistent routine. To remember and enforce these rules, they can use visual cues or reminders.

Uninvolved Parenting is characterized by a lack of responsiveness to a child's needs. This isn't a style that any parent should aspire to, but it's essential to be aware of how symptoms might lead to unintentional emotional neglect. Regularly scheduled quality time, reminders for important events, and mindfulness practices can help you stay engaged and present.

Authoritarian Parenting is a strict style with high expectations and low responsiveness. This style can be challenging because it requires high levels of organization and consistency. However, if you identify with this style, you can adapt it by focusing on a few key rules that they deem crucial. They can also work on expressing love and praise more frequently, counterbalancing the strictness with positive reinforcement.

Navigating Parental Guilt

Parenting guilt is that nagging feeling that creeps into our minds and hearts, convincing us that we're somehow falling short as parents. It whispers in our ears, "You could have done better," "You're not doing enough," or "You're doing it all wrong." It's that weight that sits on our chests, making us question our choices, actions, and even our love for our children.

Now, how does this guilt show up? Well, it can manifest in various ways. Sometimes, it's triggered by comparing ourselves to other parents or societal expectations. We see pictures of seemingly perfect families on social media, or we hear stories of other parents who seem to have it all figured out. And in those moments, we start questioning ourselves: "Am I doing enough? Should I be doing more?"

Parenting guilt also tends to rear its head when we make mistakes or face challenges. We're only humans, after all, and despite our best intentions, we stumble and falter along the parenting journey. Maybe we lost our temper, missed an important milestone, or couldn't attend every school event. These moments become fodder for our guilt, making us believe that we've failed our children in some way.

Another source of parenting guilt lies in the expectations we place on ourselves. We often have this unattainable vision of what it means to be a "perfect parent." We strive to be patient, always present, endlessly nurturing, and to have all the answers. But the truth is, no one can meet these lofty standards consistently. We're bound to make mistakes, get overwhelmed, or feel exhausted at times. Yet we beat ourselves up for not living up to this impossible ideal.

But why do we experience parenting guilt in the first place? It's essential to understand that guilt, to some extent, can be a natural part of parenting. We want the best for our children, and we carry the weight of responsibility on our shoulders. We fear that our actions or decisions will have a negative impact on their lives. In a way, guilt can be a sign of our deep love and dedication as parents.

Moreover, societal pressures and external expectations play a significant role. We live in a world where parenting is often judged and scrutinized. Everyone seems to have an opinion on how we should raise our children, and this constant barrage of advice can make us doubt ourselves. We question whether we're measuring up, whether we're doing enough to meet the perceived standards of "good parenting."

Here are some things that you can do to help you navigate that parenting guilt:

- **Practice Self-Compassion**: Treat yourself with kindness and understanding. Recognize that you're only human and that making mistakes is a natural part of the parenting journey. When guilt or frustration arises, remind yourself that you're doing the best you can in the given circumstances. Offer yourself the same compassion and forgiveness you would extend to a friend.

- **Set Realistic Expectations**: Understand that there is no such thing as a perfect parent. Let go of the unrealistic expectations you may have placed on yourself. Embrace the concept of "good enough" parenting, where you focus on providing love, care, and support to your child rather than striving for unattainable ideals. Adjust your expectations to align with your unique circumstances and your child's individual needs.

- **Seek Support**: Reach out to your support network, whether it's friends, family, or other parents who can relate to your experiences. Share your challenges, fears, and frustrations with those who can offer empathy and understanding. Connecting with others who have faced similar struggles can provide validation and a sense of solidarity, reminding you that you're not alone in your journey.

- **Educate Yourself**: Knowledge is power. Take the time to learn about your child's specific needs. Understanding their challenges and strengths can help you make informed decisions and develop strategies that work best for them. Stay updated on the latest research, resources, and therapies that can support your child's development. The more informed you are, the more confident you'll feel about your parenting choices.

- **Practice Self-Care**: Remember that taking care of yourself is essential for being a present and supportive parent. Prioritize self-care activities that rejuvenate and recharge you. It could be as simple as taking a walk in nature, reading a book, engaging in a hobby, or seeking professional help if needed. When you invest in your well-being, you enhance your capacity to handle parenting challenges and reduce feelings of guilt and frustration.

Building Positive Connections With Our Children

Building a positive relationship with our children is crucial, especially when parenting with ADHD. It sets the foundation for a healthy and supportive environment that allows both the child and the parent to thrive. So, let's dive into why fostering a positive relationship with our children is so important and explore some practical ways to build and nurture those connections.

First and foremost, a positive parent-child relationship acts as a solid emotional anchor for children. When children feel loved, understood, and valued by their parents, they develop a strong sense of self-worth and security. This foundation of trust and connection helps them navigate the ups and downs of life with greater resilience and confidence.

For parents with ADHD, building a positive relationship with their children can be particularly important. ADHD can bring its own set of challenges, such as difficulty with focus, impulsivity, and organization. But by establishing a positive bond with our children, we create an environment where our strengths can shine and compensate for the challenges we may face.

Now, let's explore some practical strategies to foster a positive relationship with our children:

- **Active Listening**: Take the time to actively listen to your child. Put away distractions, maintain eye contact, and show genuine interest in what they have to say. This simple act conveys that their thoughts and feelings are important, and it strengthens the parent-child connection.

- **Quality Time**: Set aside dedicated quality time with your child on a regular basis. Engage in activities that your child enjoys, whether it's playing games, going for walks, or pursuing shared hobbies. This focused attention demonstrates your commitment to building a positive relationship.

- **Clear Communication**: Be open and honest with your child, using age-appropriate language. Encourage them to express their thoughts and emotions, and validate their feelings. When conflicts arise, strive for constructive dialogue and find solutions together. Effective communication builds trust and understanding.

- **Consistency and Boundaries**: Establish consistent rules and boundaries in your parenting approach. Children thrive when they have clear expectations and guidelines. However, remember to balance structure with flexibility, as rigid rules can hinder the development of a positive relationship.

- **Celebrate Achievements**: Acknowledge and celebrate your child's accomplishments, whether big or small. Recognize their efforts and strengths to boost their self-esteem. A positive and encouraging atmosphere motivates children to explore their potential and fosters a sense of pride.

- **Practice Self-Care**: Taking care of your own well-being is essential for building a positive relationship with your child. Prioritize self-care and manage your ADHD symptoms through strategies like medication, therapy, exercise, and healthy routines. By taking care of yourself, you can be more present and engaged with your child.

Parental Self-Care

The saying, "You cannot pour from an empty cup," holds immense truth when it comes to balancing self-care and family responsibilities. As parents, especially those with ADHD, it's crucial to understand that taking care of ourselves is not selfish but rather a necessary foundation for effectively caring for our families. Let's delve into why finding this balance is so important and explore strategies to achieve it.

Imagine a scenario where you constantly pour all your energy and attention into your family's needs without replenishing your own resources. Over time, you'll likely find yourself feeling exhausted, overwhelmed, and emotionally drained. This can lead to decreased patience, increased stress, and even burnout, making it more challenging to meet your family responsibilities effectively.

By prioritizing self-care, you replenish your own cup, ensuring that you have the physical, emotional, and mental resources needed to tackle the demands of parenting and family life. It's like refueling your energy reserves, allowing you to show up as your best self for your children and loved ones.

So, how can you strike a balance between self-care and family responsibilities? Here are some strategies to consider:

- **Start by becoming aware of your own needs and desires**. Understand that taking care of yourself is not a luxury but a necessity. Reflect on activities, hobbies, or practices that energize and rejuvenate you. This self-awareness sets the stage for prioritizing self-care.

- **Set clear boundaries around your time and commitments**. Learn to say no when necessary, and don't feel guilty about it. By respecting your own boundaries, you create space for self-care without feeling overwhelmed by excessive responsibilities.

- **Delegate and seek support**: Don't hesitate to ask for help and share responsibilities with your partner, family members, or trusted friends. Remember, you don't have to do everything on your own. Delegating tasks lightens your load, freeing up time for self-care.

- **Treat self-care as an essential appointment on your calendar**. Block out dedicated time for activities that nourish and recharge you. Whether it's taking a walk, reading a book, practicing mindfulness, or pursuing a hobby, prioritize these moments and honor them as you would any other commitment.

- **Incorporate small self-care rituals into your daily routine**. These can be short breaks to practice deep breathing, stretching, or engaging in a mindfulness exercise. Even a few minutes of intentional self-care can have a significant impact on your well-being.

- **Include your children in your self-care activities when appropriate**. This can be as simple as taking a nature walk together, cooking a healthy meal as a family, or having a dance party in the living room. Involving your children not only allows you to spend quality time with them but also models the importance of self-care.

Remember, finding a balance between self-care and family responsibilities is an ongoing process that requires self-awareness, flexibility, and self-compassion. It's not about striving for perfection but rather making intentional choices to prioritize your well-being alongside your family's needs. By filling your own cup, you'll have more to give to your loved ones, creating a harmonious and fulfilling family dynamic.

As we're about to close off this chapter, I want to leave you with this heartfelt reminder. A reminder that you are an incredible parent doing the very best they can with the resources that they have:

Dear parent with ADHD,

You're doing a great job, and you're remarkable in the sense that you face unique challenges every day with unwavering strength and determination. Parenting is already a demanding journey, but when you add ADHD to the mix, it can feel like an uphill battle at times. Yet, despite the obstacles you encounter, you continue to show up for your children with boundless love and care. That, in itself, is truly remarkable.

Parenting with ADHD requires an extraordinary level of self-awareness and a deep understanding of your own strengths and weaknesses. But let me assure you, your children benefit immensely from having you as their parent. Your ADHD brings with it a unique perspective and a creativity that allows you to see the world through a different lens. You may find unconventional solutions to problems, think outside the box, and embrace spontaneity in ways that others can't. Your vibrant energy and enthusiasm can ignite a sense of wonder and curiosity in your children, inspiring them to explore the world with an open mind.

It's important to remember that ADHD is not a limitation; it's just a different way of being. By embracing your own journey and sharing it with your children, you teach them the invaluable lessons of acceptance and self-love. You show them that everyone's path is unique and that our differences should be celebrated rather than shunned.

In the midst of the chaos, don't forget to celebrate your victories, no matter how small they may seem. Your ability to adapt, persevere, and find joy in the little moments is a testament to your resilience. You're teaching your children the importance of resilience and the power of a positive mindset—lessons that will serve them well throughout their lives.

So, as you navigate the challenging and rewarding world of parenting, always remember that you are enough. Your love, dedication, and unique perspective make you an incredible parent, and your children are so incredibly lucky to have you in their lives.

Conclusion

Here we are at this point—the end, but not so much the end. Maybe you're reading this and telling yourself that there's still so much you need to teach yourself and a lot of grace you have yet to learn to give yourself. Maybe you're thinking that there's still a lot that you need to learn to accept about your ADHD. But let me tell you this: you are not alone. There are millions of women out there, just like you, who are grappling with the same feelings, the same worries, and the same hopes. Every day, they wake up and try to understand this complex, often misunderstood world of ADHD.

ADHD is not a defect, nor is it a shortcoming. It's merely a different way of experiencing the world. And that experience, with all its highs and lows, is a part of who you are. It's woven into the fabric of your being; it colors your perceptions, and it fuels your creativity. It's what makes you unique, distinct, and irreplaceable.

Remember, the journey of understanding and accepting your ADHD is not a race; it's a marathon. It's okay to take your time to stumble or fall. What matters is that you get up, dust yourself off, and keep going. It's okay to not have all the answers and to still be learning and growing. That's what life is all about.

In your hands, you have the power to shape your ADHD into a tool for understanding, for growth, and for resilience. Use it to carve out a space for yourself in this world, a space where you can breathe, thrive, and shine in all your brilliant uniqueness.

As we close this book, remember that this is not the end. Rather, it's the beginning of a new chapter in your life, a chapter filled with self-discovery, acceptance, and self-love. Embrace your ADHD. Embrace yourself. Because you, my dear reader, are extraordinary, just the way you are.

May your journey be filled with courage, strength, and an unshakeable belief in yourself. You are not just surviving with ADHD; you are thriving. And that is the most beautiful thing of all.

Thank You!

Thank you for purchasing **ADHD Women & Relationships!** Your support means the world.

As a token of our appreciation, scan the QR code below to download the **Laugh-a-licious Workbook Companion**—your fun partner in self-discovery and growth!

We hope this workbook brings you joy! If you have any questions or want to stay updated, feel free to reach out at hello@ivycastillo.com

We'd Love Your Feedback!

If you enjoyed the book, please consider leaving a review. Your thoughts help us and guide others to valuable insights.

Thank you for being part of our community!

References

8 ways to strengthen a parent-child relationship. (2020, July 28). Family Services. https://www.familyservicesnew.org/news/8-ways-to-strengthen-a-parent-child-relationship/

Adult attention-deficit/hyperactivity disorder (ADHD) - symptoms and causes. (2019, June 22). Mayo Clinic. https://www.mayoclinic.org/diseases-conditions/adult-adhd/symptoms-causes/syc-20350878

Atwell, E. (2017, August 28). *The hidden struggles of a woman with ADHD.* Healthline. https://www.healthline.com/health/hidden-struggles-of-a-woman-with-adhd

Building a great relationship with your child. Laura markham. (n.d.). Aha! Parenting.com. https://www.ahaparenting.com/read/building-relationship

Blomquist, L. (2022, Summer 12). *5 ways to practice empathy in your relationship.* Brides. https://www.brides.com/practice-empathy-in-relationship-6951684

Brady, K. (2019, June 5). *5 types of boundaries for your relationship.* Keir Brady Counseling Services. https://keirbradycounseling.com/relationship-boundaries/

Burton, N. (2020, November 2). Self-care strategies *for parents when you have no time for yourself.* Healthline. https://www.healthline.com/health/parenting/self-care-strategies-for-parents-no-time

Caron, C. (2022, February 18). *A.D.H.D. can strain relationships. Here's how couples cope.* The New York Times. https://www.nytimes.com/2022/02/18/well/mind/adhd-dating-relationships.html

Couples Therapy. (2022, April 27). *6 steps to navigate ADHD in your relationship*. Connect Couples Therapy & Marriage Counseling. https://connectcouplestherapy.com/6-steps-to-navigate-adhd-in-your-relationship/

Cox, J. (2022, October 31). *ADHD and sexless marriage: Causes and what to do*. Psych Central. https://psychcentral.com/adhd/adhd-and-sexless-marriage

Crawford, N. (2003, February). *ADHD: A women's issue*. APA. *https://Www.apa.org*. https://www.apa.org/monitor/feb03/adhd

Cummins, M. (2023, January 12). *How ADHD adults keep conversations from going horribly wrong*. Marla Cummins. https://marlacummins.com/adhd-communication-problems/

Davenport, B. (2020, May 31). *21 examples of healthy boundaries in relationships*. Live Bold and Bloom. https://liveboldandbloom.com/05/relationships/healthy-boundaries-in-relationships

Deadwiler, A. (2020, June 24). *Every relationship needs these 4 types of intimacy (beyond the physical)*. Mindbodygreen. https://www.mindbodygreen.com/articles/types-of-intimacy-besides-sex

Embrace your unique brilliance: Thriving with ADHD! (n.d). Cognitively. https://cognitively.co.uk/blogs/news/embrace-your-unique-brilliance-thriving-with-adhd

5 Ways to help children build positive relationships. (n.d.) Big Life Journal. https://biglifejournal.com/blogs/blog/help-children-build-positive-relationships

Jones, B. (2023, April 5). *Intimacy: Types, examples, and overcoming fears*. Verywell Health. https://www.verywellhealth.com/intimacy-7253066#:~:text=There%20are%20five%20types%20of

July 21, E. Y., & 2021. (2023, March 1). *This is what it looks like to set personal and emotional boundaries*. Real Simple.

https://www.realsimple.com/health/mind-mood/emotional-health/how-to-set-boundaries

Klein, A. (2021, April 7). *Dating someone with ADHD? 10 ways to be supportive.* Healthline. https://www.healthline.com/health/adhd/dating-someone-with-adhd

Littmann, E. (2023, June 5). *Gender differences in ADHD: Why women struggle more.* Attitude Mag. https://www.additudemag.com/gender-differences-in-adhd-women-vs-men/#:~:text=Compared%20to%20men%2C%20women%20with

Manipod, V. (2019, May 28). *Debunking 5 common misconceptions about ADHD.* Healthline. https://www.healthline.com/health/mental-health/adhd-myths-debunked

Marie, S. (2022, August 26). *Misunderstanding in a relationship: 9 tips for better communication.* Psych Central. https://psychcentral.com/relationships/pointers-for-couples-to-prevent-resolve-misunderstandings

Martin, S. (2020, April 23). *7 types of boundaries you may need.* Psych Central. https://psychcentral.com/blog/imperfect/2020/04/7-types-of-boundaries-you-may-need

MB.BCh, S. A. (2021, July 1). *Council post: The importance of setting healthy boundaries.* Forbes. https://www.forbes.com/sites/forbescoachescouncil/2021/07/01/the-importance-of-setting-healthy-boundaries/?sh=2e65c22b56e4

Miller, G. (2021, July 22). *ADHD Parenting: 12 tips to tackle common challenges.* Psych Central. https://psychcentral.com/childhood-adhd/parenting-kids-with-adhd-tips-to-tackle-common-challenges

Nassari, N. (2019, December 10). *5 conversation challenges with ADHD — and tips for better communication*. Teva.SCS.Life Effects. https://www.tevapharm.com/patients-and-caregivers/five-conversation-challenges-with-adhd-and-tips-for-better-communication/

Pattanaik, S. (n.d.). *Why boundaries are important in relationships and how to set them effectively?* LinkedIn. https://www.linkedin.com/pulse/why-boundaries-important-relationships-how-set-them-pattanaik/

Pattemore, C. (2021, June 3). *10 ways to build and preserve better boundaries*. Psych Central. https://psychcentral.com/lib/10-way-to-build-and-preserve-better-boundaries

Perera, M. (2018, April 18). *Dr mahendra perera – top 10 challenges faced by adults with ADHD*. Mahendraperera.com. https://mahendraperera.com/top-10-challenges-faced-by-adults-with-adhd/

Porter, E. (2017, October 13). *Parenting tips for ADHD: Do's and don'ts*. Healthline Media. https://www.healthline.com/health/adhd/parenting-tips

Pugle, M. (2022, June 6). *8 myths and facts about ADHD*. Everyday Health https://www.everydayhealth.com/adhd/myths-about-adhd-debunked/

Ramesy, R. (2022, March 12). *Adult ADHD and Neuro-intimacy in Couples*. Psychology Today https://www.psychologytoday.com/intl/blog/rethinking-adult-adhd/202203/adult-adhd-and-neuro-intimacy-in-couples

Schrijver, J. (2021, April 2). *ADHD and communication difficulties in adults: causes + tips*. Wandering Minds. https://wanderingminds.world/en/adhd-communication-difficulties-adults/

Schwartz, D. (2021, July 21). *The Importance of Self-Care for Parents*. Psychology Today.

https://www.psychologytoday.com/intl/blog/adolescents-explained/202107/the-importance-self-care-parents

Scott, E. (2022, January 25). *How to improve your relationships with effective communication skills.* Verywell Mind. https://www.verywellmind.com/managing-conflict-in-relationships-communication-tips-3144967

Sinfield , J. (2023, October 17). *How women can still have a great life with ADHD.* Verywell Mind. https://www.verywellmind.com/tips-for-women-with-adhd-4062682

T. Hyatt, V. (2012, December 18). *How ADHD affects relationships and what you can do.* Healthline. https://www.healthline.com/health/adhd/adult-adhd-relationships

18 symptoms that could indicate adult ADHD. (2022, October 20) Cleveland Clinic. https://health.clevelandclinic.org/adhd-symptoms-in-adults/

Taylor, J., & Ph.D. (2008, July 18). *13 survival strategies for moms with ADHD.* ADDitude. https://www.additudemag.com/when-moms-have-adhd-too/

Waters, S. (2022, April 13). *Healthy boundaries in relationships: A guide for building and keeping.* Better Up https://www.betterup.com/blog/healthy-boundaries-in-relationships

Made in United States
Cleveland, OH
06 June 2025

17518235R00085